PRAISE FOR

The Strawberry Letter

"This book, honestly, is fantastic."

—KATHIE LEE GIFFORD, *Today*

"Like that reliable friend who's always there for you . . . *The Strawberry Letter* doesn't disappoint."

—*Essence*

"Shirley digs through her own experiences with bad relationships to inspire readers with her love and marriage tips."

—*Sister 2 Sister*

"Strawberry is spreading her pearls of wisdom in . . . this book [that] offers advice with a heaping side of love. [She] is your best friend giving you good advice on how to stop, listen, and overcome . . . timely and on point with its meaningful messages and warm wisdom."

—*Los Angeles Sentinel*

"Her honesty and accountability regarding the wrong turns she's made over the course of her life are worthy of an ovation. . . . The manner in which she assumes responsibility and how she rose above her bad decisions is freeing and creates an indelible connection between Strawberry and the reader. Her dual perspective of single parenthood particularly stands out."

—*The St. Louis American*

"There's something about Shirley Strawberry that makes people want to stop and hear what she has to say."

—Washington *Afro-American*

"It's not just a relationship book . . . it's tips on how to have a happier life."

—EURWeb

"Helpful suggestions for a drama-loving girlfriend . . . This book is full of short gems that provide welcome advice on the run."

—*New York Amsterdam News*

"Only a woman who lives life with purpose and divine revelation can inspire people through her advice, and that is Shirley."

—TYLER PERRY, writer/director/producer

"Shirley Strawberry is a sistah who has been there and conquered that. Her insightful advice on life, love, and relationships makes her book a must-read for anyone struggling with past hurts."

—MO'NIQUE, Academy Award winner and host of *The Mo'Nique Show*

"Shirley Strawberry has a gift that both men and women will appreciate. She keeps it real with the ladies, while giving brothers valuable insight into the mind of a woman."

—WILL PACKER, producer, *Takers, Obsessed,* and *This Christmas*

"Shirley Strawberry brings a unique blend of experiential wisdom and compassionate insight wrapped in a package of dialogue that is painfully honest and joyfully helpful. She has that rare spiritual ability to 'speak the truth in love' while making you laugh at the same time."

—BISHOP KENNETH C. ULMER, Faithful Central Bible Church, Los Angeles

"Shirley's book provides valuable insight into the dynamics of building a great relationship, repairing broken relationships, and abandoning oppressive relationships. Her advice should be followed by all who seek real love."

—JUDGE GREG MATHIS, host of *The Judge Mathis Show*

"The Strawberry Letter is the best thing that Shirley could've ever done for my life. After I read this book and took that real talk, with that real advice, I'm no longer bitter. I'm sexy now! She's the Oprah of radio!"

—SHERYL UNDERWOOD, comedienne and president of
Zeta Phi Beta Sorority, Inc.

"Every woman in any relationship, good or bad, should read this book, and then buy one for her significant other. This is not the Bible, but Shirley has certainly provided words to live by."

—GEORGE WALLACE, comedian

"Insightful, authentic, and *loving* are just a few words that come to mind when I think of Shirley Strawberry. She's wise beyond her years and has the gift of connecting with her audience regardless of their age or circumstance. In this book, she speaks from the heart and gives honest, nonjudgmental straight talk to her readers."

—WENDY RAQUEL ROBINSON, actress, *The Game*

"Shirley Strawberry is a real sister-girlfriend who tells you what you *need* to know, even when it's not what you *want* to know."

—TERRI J. VAUGHN, actress, *Meet the Browns*

The
Strawberry Letter

The
Strawberry Letter

REAL TALK, REAL ADVICE,
BECAUSE BITTERNESS ISN'T SEXY

SHIRLEY STRAWBERRY

WITH LYAH BETH LeFLORE

ONE WORLD TRADE PAPERBACKS | BALLANTINE BOOKS | NEW YORK

2012 One World Trade Paperback Edition

Published in the United States by One World Books,
an imprint of The Random House Publishing Group,
a division of Random House, Inc., New York.

ONE WORLD is a registered trademark and the One World
colophon is a trademark of Random House, Inc.

Originally published in hardcover in the United States by
One World Books, an imprint of The Random House Publishing Group,
a division of Random House, Inc., in 2011.

Library of Congress Cataloging-in-Publication Data

Strawberry, Shirley.
The strawberry letter : real talk, real advice, because bitterness isn't sexy /
Shirley Strawberry with Lyah Beth LeFlore.
p. cm.
ISBN 978-0-345-52551-2
eBook ISBN 978-0-345-52552-9
1. Interpersonal relations. 2. Women—Conduct of life. 3. Man-woman
relationships. I. LeFlore, Lyah Beth. II. Title.
HM1106.S775 2011
646.70082—dc22
2011000551

Printed in the United States of America

www.oneworldbooks.net

2 4 6 8 9 7 5 3 1

Book design by Caroline Cunningham

To the woman who gave birth to me, and who now helps me raise my own daughter, my beautiful mother, Ms. Helen Louise Clark. Thank you for everything. I love you, Mom!

FOREWORD

Host of The Steve Harvey Morning Show

I've been Shirley's partner in radio for over ten years now, and during that time I've gotten to know her quite well. And I can tell you she is one of the most fascinating and spiritually blessed people I've ever met. I am amazed by how she manages to balance her personal and professional life—especially as a single mother. Just because she hasn't discovered Mr. Right has not stopped her from growing and developing as a person. In fact, it's given her an even more interesting perspective.

"The Strawberry Letter" is one of our most popular features on the show. Shirley's advice is the more sensible approach, quite contrary to what my answers are, which are really always to the left. I think a lot of the women, and men too, who read this book will discover that her advice comes from some of her own experiences—as a mother, a professional, a single woman, and a friend. As you read this book, and you take the trip that Shirley sends you on, it's gonna make you think. You may read one of the letters and say, "Wow, this actually happened to someone?" You'll find yourself wondering what you would do if you were in that same situation or how it could have been avoided in the first place.

Our segment "The Strawberry Letter" has become an entertaining teaching tool. I think Shirley's advice and the life lessons she shares with you in *The Strawberry Letter* are going to give people a view into themselves, their neighbors, their friends, their families; anyone who may have similar issues.

And I guarantee, you may not find yourself in *all* of these letters, but you *know* someone in these Strawberry Letters, no matter how crazy the situations are. You're gonna be able to take these letters and Shirley's experiences and advice and apply them to your daily lives, and I know it's going to work out really well for you as a result.

This all takes me back to when Shirley and I first started on the show together. Truthfully, I was uncomfortable with her. See, I was this rebel guy, and I didn't really care for Shirley being on the show—after all, I started the show by myself. I remember during those first three days, I didn't think she was a good idea *at all*. The station brought her in to be a voice of reason on the show, but it really was to teach me radio. I actually had no idea how the day-to-day tasks of the show were supposed to go.

Finally, she just grew on me. I started to like her, because she didn't have a very aggressive approach, but she managed to get her point across. She would say, "Okay, Steve, this is what you're *supposed* to do. Now, you can do what you *wanna* do, but this is how you're *supposed* to do it." She left the final decision up to me. At the same time, she found a way to get some of the stuff on the radio that management wanted. Then I really started to understand what she did and her value, and that I needed a partner on the show who had a sound voice.

And while our relationship started out as a professional one, over the course of time she's become my friend. In fact, she's one of the few female friends I have. I've never really been good at developing friendships with women. If I was talking to a woman, it was because I was dating her. I didn't really know *how* to be a woman's friend. But Shirley's been with me through some of the lowest moments in my life. Through my divorce, when my father and my brother passed. I've been through a lot, and in those dark hours Shirley's always given me solid advice.

She's incredibly loyal, too. No matter what people have said about me, she has defended me. When negative stuff was out there on the Internet, or in the media, she brought it to my attention. She would say, "Steve, people who really know you know how you are, but most important God knows you. Don't get down because some blogger said something about you. They don't even know you." She's kind of built me up over the years and I've always appreciated that.

She's one of the kindest, most spiritual people I know—that's real. She will admit when she has a fault and that makes it okay for me to show mine to her. She laughs at me. She laughs with me. She has cried with me. All of it, and it's truly because she cares as a person. And that caring, sharing, good-hearted perspective is exactly what you will find in *The Strawberry Letter*. So I hope you enjoy this book as much as I've enjoyed sitting next to Shirley over the years.

CONTENTS

FOREWORD: *by Steve Harvey*   IX

INTRODUCTION: *Turn My Mic Up!*   XVII

PART ONE

Woman To Woman: Taking Inventory

CHAPTER 1   *Get Out of Your Comfort Zone*   3

CHAPTER 2   *Sisterhood*   13

CHAPTER 3   *Stay Ready*   20

PART TWO

Love and Relationships: The Joy and the Pain

CHAPTER 4 Stop Being Stuck on Stupid   27

CHAPTER 5 Bad Boys, Bad Boys, Whatcha Gonna Do?   33

CHAPTER 6 What a Girl Wants   42

CHAPTER 7 Lashes, Lipstick, & Stilettos   50

CHAPTER 8 Yours, Mine, Ours   54

CHAPTER 9 Clean Up Your Act   58

CHAPTER 10 What Did You Say?   64

CHAPTER 11 No Finance = No Romance   72

CHAPTER 12 Stay on Your Game   77

CHAPTER 13 Shame on You, Shame on Me   82

CHAPTER 14 Security, Please   87

CHAPTER 15 Losing It   91

CHAPTER 16 Bitterness Isn't Sexy   98

PART THREE

Family Matters: God Bless the Child

CHAPTER 17 It Takes a Woman!   105

CHAPTER 18 The Ties That Bind   113

CHAPTER 19 Make the Grade   118

CHAPTER 20 Stop the Madness   123

PART FOUR

Self: No More Drama

CHAPTER 21   *Pass the Torch*   129

CHAPTER 22   *Do You Like What You See?*   134

CHAPTER 23   *Where Is Your Faith?*   137

EPILOGUE: *Shirley's Strawberry Letter to Self*   140

BONUS: *More of "The Strawberry Letter"!*   143

ACKNOWLEDGMENTS   159

INTRODUCTION

Turn My Mic Up!

Steve Harvey and I have been giving advice on his radio show through "The Strawberry Letter" for more than ten years. It started in Los Angeles when our show was local. We decided to have an advice column based on my last name and the Brothers Johnson classic hit "Strawberry Letter 23," and it grew into a life of its own and is now one of the most popular features on *The Steve Harvey Morning Show*. Some of the letters, as you'll see in the book, are tame and straight to the point. Others are just plain crazy and totally strain believability—husbands cheating over the Internet, women sleeping with their stepsons, women sleeping with their daughters-in-law, jealous boyfriends, crazy mothers-in-law, out-of-control baby mamas, and triflin' baby daddies. People always ask, "Do you make these letters up?" and I tell them that although I have a very active imagination, there is no way I could make this stuff up. These letters are very real.

When I first started doing "The Strawberry Letter" I didn't think people wanted to hear what I had to say, but ten years and nearly eight million listeners later, it's clear. It's crazy, because I didn't set out to give advice like this; I just wanted to be part of a great radio show. Who knew that people would be so affected by the letters? Every morning they wait for "The Strawberry Letter" (or "The Letter," as we like to call it). If they're in their cars, listening before work, they won't get out until we're done. If they're at work, they turn their radios up when "The Letter" comes on.

Whenever Steve and I travel around the country, our listeners tell me how much they love the show, and *especially* the letters. So many people have asked me to write a book, or they'll say, "When's your book coming out, Shirley?" They hear me talk about my own struggles in relationships, and the fact that I've been single for some years. Occasionally, I get a comment like "I don't get it. Why aren't you in a relationship?"

Good question, because currently I'm not dating. I think that's a pretty known fact among our listeners. The right man just hasn't come along yet. The Bible says, *"He who findeth a wife findeth a good thing."* I'm confident and faithful he'll find me.

Some might say, "You're single, with no man, how can you give advice?" I say *that's exactly* why. I've been in enough bad relationships to know how to avoid them! I look at it like this:

some people are better coaches than players. My advice is based on life experience and plain common sense.

My ex-husband and I dated for about a year before we got married. I can honestly say that knowing what I know now, all the signs were there that the marriage wasn't going to last. I knew a few months into it that I had made the biggest mistake of my life. I got pregnant a year and a half later and stayed with him off and on for years after that, trying to make the marriage work. It was hard, but I'm glad that part of my life is behind me, and I can honestly say we're friends now. Plus, I got a great last name and a lovely daughter out of it! So, why complain?

I'm that candid about my life, and I've learned from our listeners that they appreciate my honesty and ability to connect with them. Therefore, in response to women from all walks of life who are just like me, and who love "The Strawberry Letter," I finally decided to take the next step and write a book, *The Strawberry Letter*.

I was further motivated to represent for the ladies after having the incredible opportunity to work with Steve Harvey, and be an instrumental sounding board and contributor on both his books.

I'm especially grateful to Steve for writing his first book, *Act Like a Lady, Think Like a Man*. I have to say, I owe him such a debt of gratitude. I may have taught him radio, but he teaches me so much more about life and men. I'm often asked what it's like to work with him. I tell people that it's great and a crazy adventure every day. I'm so inspired by him. Thank you, Steve! Now here I am writing my own book!

The Strawberry Letter, the book, is semi-autobiographical, and you'll see some of our listeners' favorite Strawberry Letters as I explore aspects of dating, marriage, and divorce; single parenting; battles with self-esteem and self-love and how that transfers into not just our personal lives, but our professional lives as well.

The book is divided into four parts, which I think shape and drive the core of who we are as women. Part One, Woman to Woman, is more like a "call to action," to help the reader take inventory of her life, personally and professionally. Parts Two and Three cover the most popular topics that fans seek advice about: love and relationships and family. In Love and Relationships, we get to the heart and soul of the often complex and frustrating world of dating, marriage, and life after a breakup or divorce. You will find Family Matters to be a powerful and very personal segment of the book. For so many of the show's fans who are single mothers like me, our families are top priority and sometimes we just need to know that we aren't in it alone. Finally, in the fourth part of the book, Self, the life lessons come full circle, from battling with and overcoming self-esteem issues and depression, to finding balance and living a spiritually rich and faith-filled life.

Some of the chapters begin with actual Strawberry Letters—some of the most popular—from the show and throughout the book, each chapter ends with what I call a Strawberry Tip—personal anecdotes that I want you to refer to whenever you need some advice on the run, a quick emotional pick-me-up, or help for your drama-struck girlfriend. I suggest using them, like I do, as part of your daily motivational mantra. You could even copy them and tape them to your bathroom mirror.

Finally, the book concludes with a Strawberry Letter to myself, followed by a special treat for the fans, a bonus collection of Strawberry Letters that are fan favorites. These letters are definitely some of the wildest heard on air and they still keep Steve, Carla, Nephew Tommy, and me falling out with laughter!

Ultimately, I hope that *The Strawberry Letter* will encourage you to make better choices and decisions in relationships—whether they be with your family, your lover, or in the workplace. Just like the advice we give in "The Strawberry Letter" every day on the show, my advice is authentic and raw. I've "been there and done that." I always speak directly from and to the hearts, spirits, and souls of women all over the country, hoping to help them find strength within their own lives as I have in mine.

As you apply the lessons, advice, and stories within these pages to your daily lives, remember that carrying around unhealthy baggage from your past plants the seeds that blossom into bitterness. So let's take this journey together. Be inspired. Be motivated. Be healed, reinvigorated, and challenged to love yourself and to love your life!

PART ONE

Woman to Woman

Taking Inventory

"Take some inventory of your woman and

your glory, leave the bad things behind . . ."

—ARETHA FRANKLIN

"Look Into Your Heart"

CHAPTER ONE

Get Out of Your Comfort Zone

I often wonder why some women seem to be afraid or hesitant to try new things. So many of us go to work and then come home and, well, that's it! Or we hang out with the *same* people all the time, or go have the *same* drink at the *same* bar or club. Before you know it, like a flash of light, life is going to be over. At some point you have to say, "Hey, there has to be more to life," and acknowledge that fear is holding you back. Well, it is time to erase that fear to try new things.

I wasn't always so brave, and in my case, I think that spirit of fear was passed down to me. My mother was too busy working and taking care of my brother and me to be adventurous and try new things or encourage me to develop those attributes, so it is important I break that cycle. I stretch out of my comfort zone and model that for my daughter.

I love doing things that are exhilarating and fun. This may

sound silly, but I like riding roller coasters. Think about it. As the car climbs its way up that steep and narrow hill made of tons of twisted metal and steel that stretches for what seems like miles, your pulse races as you anticipate the unexpected.

It finally inches its way to the top, and before you can blink, you're released. You drop, falling hundreds of feet toward the ground, and the adrenaline rush takes over. You don't have time to think about getting comfortable. That's what life's about, taking that leap of faith that might be uncomfortable at first, but you find yourself liking it.

I always wanted to swim and when I was working in Los Angeles I heard there was a guy in my neighborhood giving lessons. Learning to swim was a great accomplishment, but fear (and worrying about my hair!) could've kept me from taking the plunge. I remember how fast my heart was racing as my swim instructor slowly led me into the water. He kept saying, "I got you. I got you." Part of me was saying, "Are you crazy, Shirley, you could drown!"

However, as my body was submerged deeper and deeper into the water, I suddenly felt weightless. Still tightly holding my hand, my instructor told me to take a deep breath and hold it, because we were going under. My pulse was going a mile a minute. I didn't know what to expect next. Before I could even try to think about making a fast break out of the pool, he had counted to three and I was underwater.

The saltwater pool was exhilarating. My head popped back up to the surface seconds later, and I thought, Wow, what an amazing feeling. Before I knew it I was splashing around like I had been swimming my entire life. I was one with the water!

Sometimes we talk ourselves out of trying a new experience

by saying, "I can't do that. I'm too old," or "I'm too fat." There's always going to be an excuse, so we have to lay those things aside and at least be willing to try.

I read in Diana Ross's biography that if she wanted to learn about something she would take a class, and that when she walked into the classroom everyone would be shocked to see that Diana Ross was in class with them, but she didn't care. Certainly, if Diana Ross, who probably back then could barely walk out of her front door without being recognized, felt that learning was more important than any discomfort she might experience, then surely we can put our fears aside to have new experiences too.

We have to open ourselves up and broaden our horizons, step out of our comfort zone and do things we may not normally do, such as taking up golf or enrolling in a foreign language class. This is essential for our growth and survival.

I have several girlfriends who have recently taken up salsa. Dancing and good music is always great fun. I don't think we're ever too old to try something new. Try to remember those dreams you used to have and the things that made you happy, and seek those things out. Find a way to bring them back into your life. We've gotta do things we wouldn't ordinarily do or that may seem scary or stupid. Hey, I'm talking to myself as much as I'm talking to you.

Save your money, get a passport, and take a trip out of the country! And, hello! You don't have to wait for a man to take you there. Start a book club or Bible study at your home. Hey, you might even dare to gather a group of girlfriends and take a pole dancing class. I hear it's great fun! Instead of being sad and thinking about what you don't have, think about things you do have at your disposal and build on that for new experiences.

Cook a big dinner and invite your friends over who have no family. Or go old school and have a potluck dinner. Just make sure your friends can cook, though, because there's nothing worse than having a big old dinner and somebody brings an unappetizing dish and you have to pretend you like it. Do to your non-cooking girlfriends what people used to do to me when they'd say, "Shirley, just bring the soda!"

Your new attitude to venture out of the familiar could be something as simple as changing the color of polish you paint your toes. Hello, why do you have to always wear red? The next time you go to the nail shop get a French manicure. Or go hot pink with white polka dots! Look, maybe changing your polish is a baby step, *but* it's a step.

I rely on seven simple steps on a daily basis, and I pass them on to other women regularly:

1. **Look your best at all times.** Okay, ladies, at six A.M. I'm camera ready *every* day: hair, lipstick, and even lashes. I know we're on the radio and not television, and it would be very easy for me to be comfortable in sweats and no makeup. I certainly could sleep an extra thirty minutes to an hour. But when I started working with Steve I got excited about stepping up my game not only professionally, but appearance wise. I knew Steve had a reputation for being a sharp dresser. Working with a guy like him, you'd better not come in there looking crazy! Besides, I am not going to let a man be prettier than me.

2. **Be a team player.** Some days you are a standout player or captain, like a Kobe Bryant or Lebron James, and other days you have to know how to pass the ball. Prime example, I work with comedians. Sometimes I'm the butt of the joke. However, in stepping out of my comfort zone of taking myself too seriously, I've learned to take the humor in stride. You have to learn to laugh at yourself sometimes, and being on *The Steve Harvey Morning Show* team has taught me that for sure. This may sound cliché, but life's too short! Laugh often and laugh at yourself more.

   Another example of being a team player is that I'm not a very athletic person. In fact, I'm a proud "girlie girl." However, when the show partnered with Disney theme parks on an event, I tossed caution to the wind and didn't hesitate going along with zip-lining through the park's makeshift forest with the rest of the morning show gang. Can you believe it?

   On air I'm daring and outgoing, but off air I'm much more reserved and laid-back. So, joining the gang, and zipping around the Disney forest, letting loose like Steve, Tommy, and Carla, was truly a testament of me being a team player. I let my off-air personality switch places with my on-air one and it felt great!

3. **Keep yourself updated on everything from current news events to current trends, and maximize your resources.** In radio our job is to entertain and inform listeners. However, for me, it's always been about taking it to the next level. I don't just depend on getting information when I'm *on* the job. In my spare time I read books,

magazines, newspapers, and check out what's happening on the Internet. Being aware helps you to be prepared for the unexpected times when you're forced to step out of, again, your comfort zone. You never know, you may be interviewing the president of the United States one morning, just like we did recently on the show. I couldn't believe we were actually speaking with President Barack Obama!

4. **Don't be afraid to reinvent yourself, from your image to your career choice.** Hey, someone may just ask you to write a book, like me! Suddenly, I went from giving advice in the mornings with Steve Harvey to being an author. I was scared to death, but I took the challenge head on!

5. **Be both accommodating and assertive, and don't be afraid to express your ideas.** I'm pretty easygoing when I'm in the workplace. I don't mind getting Steve a cup of coffee. No, I'm not his assistant, but it doesn't degrade me as a woman, or belittle my status as his colleague and co-host to take on a task someone lower on the totem pole is expected to do. On the flip side, I'm sure that to you I'm this assertive, fearless woman dishing advice to listeners each morning. Well, believe it or not, I wasn't always that fearless when it came to The Strawberry Letter segment on the show. When I first started The Letter, I held back when it came to expressing my opinions. I simply wasn't comfortable dishing out those jagged pills to the audience. I didn't want to crush anyone's feelings. So, I used to be extra nicey-nice, borderline timid, and played it safe when answering letters. I

wasn't expressing my true feelings or opinions. But I realized after just a few months of sitting next to Steve, hearing him be so straightforward, that coming soft wasn't helping people. I wasn't being fair to the fans in need, or being true to myself. Besides, it was just my opinion. Hate it or love it, I had to keep it real. And guess what? It worked. Our listeners, even when my views were more critical, loved it. What would've happened if I had continued being afraid to speak my mind? The Strawberry Letter might not have become what it is.

6. **Do everything that's required of you and don't be afraid to go beyond expectations, because it will pay off with bigger successes in the long run.** I've always stayed at the station for as long as it takes to get the job done, with or without pay. Having that kind of reputation showed my bosses that I was the woman for the job. I moved from being an on-air personality in Chicago to a bigger market in Los Angeles, co-hosting the top morning radio show in the city, to sitting in the number two seat next to Steve Harvey there, and now being known nationally after the show was syndicated. My longevity in the business proves that not being afraid to go above and beyond what's expected pays off with bigger successes.

7. **Exercise your creative muscle outside the workplace with hobbies or other areas of interest, to alleviate stress and burnout.** Who knows? It may be the makings of your next successful career. I love interior design and clothing. So, trying out new decorating ideas at

home and fashion styling for my girlfriends is a great way to exercise and sharpen my creative muscle when I'm not working. I also love entertaining friends and family (catered of course)! Who knows, maybe a fashion/interior-decorating/entertaining show is next for me! What's *your* next successful career?

Don't let the skepticism of others stop you either. When I was just coming into adulthood I listened to other people and their negative comments. They were quick to tell me what I should and shouldn't be doing, and I'd always fall right into the negative clutches of what they had to say.

I was a smart kid and it was very unpopular to be smart where I grew up, on the south side of Chicago. But my uncle Wardell, who was my favorite uncle growing up, was really smart. He is the one who noticed that I had a great speaking voice, and that I was an exceptional reader. He would show me off in front of his friends and pick out random words and say, "This is my niece. Go on, Shirley, let them see how you can read." Once, when I was six or seven, he showed me the word "chaos," and I read it aloud, pronouncing it correctly. Everyone around was impressed and cheered me on. He grabbed me, hugged me, and spun me around.

That day probably gave him bragging rights in the neighborhood for the next month. Every time he came around he'd tell people, "I told you. Put my niece up against anyone!" He made me feel like I could do anything. My last act of gratitude was making him proud at his funeral when I read his obituary.

My uncle encouraged me to stay in school and go to college because he was a schoolteacher, but you couldn't tell me anything at that age. I *had* to have nice clothes, and in order to get that I had to work. Luckily, the opportunity in radio came along. It was at a time when you could get in the business without necessarily having a degree.

I was hardheaded back then, but thank God I eventually woke up and followed my passion. I didn't recognize it at that time, but I was in fact reaching outside of my comfort zone. I could've very easily allowed what others thought or said about me never making it in the radio business to hold me back.

The only downer was that since I made the decision to work, I didn't finish college. However, the desire for my degree is still strong in my heart.

I was in Washington, D.C., last year with the Susan G. Komen Foundation as an ambassador for breast cancer awareness. I was happy and honored to have been chosen, but I felt awkward when everyone around me talked about their college experiences and degrees. If you ask me my biggest regret, not finishing college is absolutely it. I think that's why I felt so strongly about and identified so closely with Kanye West's first album, *The College Dropout*. It's a brilliant album that felt like it mirrored my life. He's very successful, but I bet his dear mother, an educator with her doctorate degree, who has since passed away, still held on to the hope that one day he'd get his college degree.

Don't get me wrong: college isn't for everyone. There are plenty of successful people who have made it without having a college degree, but before I leave this earth, I will have my degree, and when I finally have that diploma in hand, I will probably fall on my knees. Right on the stage. And yes, I do want to walk across the stage in my cap and gown. So to people who are reading this book, know that you're never too old to get your education.

Listen up, ladies! Life has so much to offer us. Don't be sedentary and set in your ways, because the consequences may affect your spirit in ways you can't imagine.

Strawberry Tip:

Let your fears motivate you to try

new things.

CHAPTER TWO

Sisterhood

To my ladies, to my girls, to my women, there's a nasty rumor that women who work together can't get along. I don't know who put that out there. Maybe it was a man who wanted to keep us divided so he could date all of us!

It's time we show the world what we're made of. That's why I love the word "sisterhood." We don't use it enough in our daily vocabulary or carry out the spirit of it in our daily actions. It's about high-fiving another woman on a job well done, complimenting her on how amazing she looks, supporting her to be her best self, and being there for her during her low points. When we come together, we're unstoppable.

I especially admire the sacredness of our friendships with one another. Everyone will tell you that I'm a great friend. I never had any sisters, so I consider my girlfriends my sisters. I believe in sisterhood wholeheartedly and have carried that philosophy into my professional life.

One of my really good girlfriends said to me a long time ago, "Women better learn how to get along with one another, because we live longer than men. Even if we are married, usually our husbands die earlier. You've gotta have somebody to share your life with." Women share a support and deep love for one another that is unparalleled. Our connection helps us get through the good and bad times. There's nothing like hanging out and having lunch with your girlfriends, or getting respect and support from your female co-workers for your successes.

I made a conscious effort to get along with my female colleagues in the workplace, because I know the common expectation is that we won't. I feel like this: if you're confident in what you do and you have it going on in your particular area or field, then no one can take that away from you. I don't care how smart or beautiful the next woman is.

I've never allowed myself to get caught up in drama with other women at work, because I try to keep a positive attitude. There was one instance, which I'd say was more disappointing than anything.

Years ago some changes went on at the radio station at which I worked. My job was in question and other women were vying for my position. My boss told me that I didn't have to come in one particular day. I knew what was going on, but there was nothing I could do about the situation except let my work shine and speak for itself.

One woman with whom I had been very, very close wanted my job, so she went for it. She had her own agenda. Ultimately she didn't get the job, and ironically, I moved on to do something bigger and better. She later apologized to me. She told me that she'd had to think of her child. I remember saying to myself, "Okay, but I have a child too." I accepted her apology, although I was hurt at the time. I guess she felt she had to go for hers, even if it meant stepping on me to get there.

I wasn't going to backstab her, and if she won the job, she won the job. If she thought she could handle it, then God bless her. What I will say, though, is that a lot of people think they can walk in your shoes. They look at you and say, "Oh, that's not hard, I could do that." But when the deal goes down and they have to perform, they see that it's not so easy to take the crown or to move into that position.

Cathy Hughes, the founder of Radio One, is someone I looked up to even before I had the opportunity to work for her. I'm sure she had her share of struggles as a single parent and businesswoman, and that there were men—and women—who said, "Who does she think she is, trying to own all these radio stations?" She's a single parent, and I can relate to that. She often tells the story of how she was turned down by so many banks to get financing to buy her first station. Before giving up, she decided to try one more bank and they approved her. She didn't abandon her dream no matter how many doors were slammed in her face.

Imagine if she hadn't gone to that last bank? She wouldn't have the media empire she has today, and have become one of the few multimillionairesses in our field. She's an icon and a woman I admire. Over the years she's employed hundreds of women like myself who've gone on to make incredible strides and successes in radio, and now television at her own network,

TV One. She's passing the baton and epitomizes the meaning of sisterhood.

You know, I've been in the radio game a long, long time. It's a male-dominated field and I'm one of the few women still standing, which is another reason I make it a priority to develop good relationships with other women in the business. For example, I work with Carla Farrell every day and we're friends on and off air.

On air, of course, sometimes we get into it, but we can disagree without being disrespectful. We're adults. We don't have to curse each other out. I wish more women realized they don't have to go there with other women.

Carla is a very smart woman. If you ask either of us the one thing we have in common, besides our 36 DDs, it's that we both have a love for radio and radio done well. Now, on a daily basis do we see eye to eye? No, not on everything.

Her biggest problem with me right now is that she's trying to get me hooked up with a man, but she says I won't do my part. But our common goal is to help make *The Steve Harvey Morning Show* the best it can be.

That's why I salute and support my fellow sisters in radio, such as Sybil Wilkes of *The Tom Joyner Morning Show;* Dominique DiPrima and Nautica de la Cruz at KJLH in Los Angeles; Terri Avery and Chirl Girl at WBAV in Charlotte, North Carolina; Carol Blackmon at Majic 107.5 in Atlanta, Georgia; Frankie Darcell at WMXD in Detroit, Michigan; Ann Tripp at WBLS in New York; Ebony Steele on the *Ricky Smiley Morning Show;* and so many other women whom I've worked with or encountered in radio over the years.

We may even be on competing morning shows, but we all

give "love" whenever we see one another. It's about women coming together on a united front, creating networks of support, so that we can create more opportunities for one another. We can all get our shine on!

I think Steve asked me once if I got intimidated around beautiful women. I said, "Absolutely not!" I admire beauty just as he does. I will say a woman is gorgeous. Now, the only thing that might intimidate me is if she has all her educational credentials, because I don't have mine, but that just motivates me to get my act together.

If you're an older female, reach back and help some of those younger women get to where they want to be. If there's a young woman in your office who dresses inappropriately, or doesn't have proper hygiene, or is struggling with her coworkers, reach back to help her. Isn't that better than gossiping about the girl? Help this young woman be a better person—just like someone helped you, or just like you would've wanted them to when you were starting out.

And if you're a young woman, don't do like I did and act like no one can tell you anything. I thought I knew it all. Listen! Get some wisdom in your life. Go sit down with an older woman and see how she got to where she is.

Think of it this way: when you're the hot young thang on the scene and it's *all* about you, it's all good; but if you live long enough, you're gonna get older and someone else will be the new "hot young thang." I learned that from older women who looked out for me and took me under their wings when I was just starting in the business. So, realize that that kind of attention is fleeting and work to build relationships and a reputation based on substance. That's why I also encourage older women to be more open-minded when it comes to the perspective of a younger woman. Perhaps that sister's ideas are fresh and innovative and can take a project or idea to the next level. We can learn from one another.

When you generate positive energy you have an effervescent spirit and aura. Young people don't mind hanging out with you and people your age enjoy your company too. It's *all* about women creating an intergenerational bond.

Listen to young people and give them advice if they ask for it. And even if they don't—if you see them doing something they shouldn't, let them know what's on your mind in a kind way. Let them know they're going down the wrong path.

Don't let those invisible barriers—young, old, fat, skinny, tall, short—hinder how you relate or communicate to other people. There might be some days where you will have misunderstandings or not get along. Correct it immediately. Don't let it fester. Don't carry a grudge.

At the end of the day, I want women to flourish and prosper professionally and personally. I've worked hard to get to where I am in my career and if I can impart some knowledge to other women, then I'm paying it forward.

Strawberry Tip

Believe in yourself! Be confident in who you are and what you bring to the table, and if you are willing to share, know that there is more than enough for everyone.

CHAPTER THREE

Stay Ready

I love the saying "Stay ready, so you don't have to get ready." I don't know whom to attribute that quote to, but it is something that I try to live by.

Earlier this year I was asked to speak at the For Sisters Only conference sponsored by WBAV-FM in Charlotte, North Carolina. Now, even though I'm on the radio every morning, I still get nervous during public speaking engagements. People say, "How can you be so terrified when you are on the radio every morning?" They don't understand, my insecurities about not having a college degree creep in at moments like that.

Don't get me wrong, I was proud to have been asked to be the featured speaker at the conference, and impart some words of inspiration to the women attending. But I was worried and fearful that what I had to say wouldn't measure up to everyone's expectations. Whatever those expectations were. Maybe I was really more afraid that I'd disappoint myself.

In the days leading up to the event, my stomach was in knots. However, I sucked it up and buckled down and wrote my speech. The night before, I even rehearsed it several times in front of the mirror. I was finally ready. I was prepared, with my notes in hand for reference. Unfortunately, my sponsor informed me right before I went on that there was no podium. There went my notes! I was stuck. I had to just pray and get out there.

I walked onto that stage, and with each step, as I got closer and closer to the mic, I felt the panic working its way up my legs, to my stomach. But I had to keep pushing. . . .

The fear pulled at my gut. My heart was racing, pounding through my chest. I imagined myself turning around and running right off that stage. But when I reached the mic stand and looked out over the crowd of faces, something happened. It was mostly women, and a few handsome men, smiling back at me, clapping enthusiastically. They were eager to hear what I had to say.

I took a deep breath, suddenly realizing the power of the gift God had blessed me with. You know, sometimes it takes being thrust into the fire for us to have what Oprah calls an "aha moment." I began silently chanting that all too familiar phrase, "Stay ready, so you don't have to get ready!" to myself.

I quickly decided to review some random tidbits and facts about Charlotte I had jotted down on a notepad tucked away in my bag. Before I go into a city I do a bit of research because I like to be able to connect on some level with the people in that area. Sharing the simple, fun facts I found helped me to loosen up and engage my audience. You're never too old or too high up the success ladder to do your homework. I was finally relaxed and ready.

Before I knew it I had opened my mouth and the words began to flow, and then there was more applause. By the time I finished, people were standing on their feet. It was a huge success. So many women in the audience, and a few men too, came up to me afterward, telling me what an inspiration I was to them—and of course, how much they love "The Strawberry Letter" on the show.

That day I couldn't defer to my crutch, the speech I had prepared. I had to get out there, grab the microphone, stand in front of all those people, and just start talking. And guess what? That's just what I did. I can't tell you how many times God has gotten me out of a bad or scary situation. I just say, "C'mon Lord, we've gotta do this together."

You've gotta be a fighter during the scary times in this life. Be strong as it relates to everything you want. And part of being a fighter means getting ready and being prepared for whatever your personal demons may be, which for me were a fear of public speaking and my insecurities about my lack of a college degree. But a lot of times we are too busy fighting with ourselves to do battle with the outside forces that threaten to take us down. Oh, sure, I fight with Steve, Tommy, and even my brother, but my biggest fight is with Shirley Strawberry. She's on one shoulder telling me that I can't do something, and on the other saying, "Yes, you can!"

So that's why I say go for your dreams, no matter how big or lofty they may seem to others. Stop beating yourself up, or letting others bring you down. If you wanna start a business, start a business. If you need to borrow money to do it, take out a loan. Don't be afraid to walk into the bank and ask those people for some money. If they say no, there are other banks as you saw from the Cathy Hughes story I shared in a previous chapter. But be ready. Do your research, think five steps ahead, and have a plan A, B, and C.

I've had some great role models in my life. In my twenties I had some fabulous women at the first station I worked at in Chicago who, I could look up to and say, "Wow, I want to look like that! She looks amazing. She's well dressed, and well spoken. She's got class. She's comfortable with herself. She's cool." Those were the images I had in my head, and that's the kind of legacy I want to leave for the younger women coming behind me.

I have a friend who is the same age as me and she just started running marathons again, something she used to do in her twenties. As a matter of fact, she recently completed the Chicago marathon—all 26.2 miles! Now, she's so very serious about it and it gives her such a sense of pride. She trains, eats right, and gets herself ready to meet her goal. Society may try to count you out at a certain age or if you have an extra twenty or thirty pounds on you, but you can prove all the naysayers wrong.

Do whatever you can to stay in the race. That way you'll always *be* ready! It would be so easy to just quit and let everybody else have what you think you don't deserve. But why? Why do that? You've got to keep on moving and pushing. Yes, it gets tiring and some days you want to give up. But it's all about self-motivation. Fight on!

Strawberry Tip:

Keep running life's marathons!

PART TWO

Love and Relationships

The Joy and the Pain

"How come the things that make us happy

make us sad . . ."

—FRANKIE BEVERLY AND MAZE

"Joy and Pain"

CHAPTER FOUR

Stop Being Stuck on Stupid

SUBJECT: Tell Me What I Want to Hear

I am old enough to know better, but I don't want to be by myself. I met a man who I liked very much. He would leave his family for a couple of days at a time and spend that time with me. I fell in love with him. He would tell me his wife did not make love to him. She did not cook enough, and the only thing she did was spend money. So I stepped in and did the things she wouldn't. We moved in together, but now I have realized his wife did not make love to him because he was sleeping with me. She had food on the table, but he wasn't home to eat it. The money she spent was to take care of the family (mortgage, food, insurance, car payments). Now I feel like a fool. The only thing I got was a broke man who doesn't have a pot to piss in. He is always mad and misses his family, therefore, we do not have sex and my happy

home has become a broke-down shack. What do I do now? I thought
the grass was greener on the other side. WHAT A FOOL I AM!

This woman is being very stupid, and the bad thing is, she
knows it. You would think that would make it clear to her
what she needs to do. Unfortunately, she seems to be stuck in
a bad way. Listen, what married man doesn't say that there's
trouble at home when he's chasing after another woman?
That's how they get in. The problem with her is that she was
so desperate, she believed it.

This is the perfect example of the grass not being greener
on the other side. And for those of us who still think it is, this
letter certainly proves that it's not. It never is. So many times
we want to have something better than what we've got, which
means we're not appreciating what we do have. Even though
this woman was alone and single, she soon found out that
being with a married man who treated her like crap just to
have a man in her life was way worse than her current situation. She'd better ask him to leave if she wants her life to
change. Immediately! And if he doesn't leave, kick his butt
out—anything less than that is just plain stupid.

I hate to say it, but ladies, sometimes we get stuck on stupid
and can't get up. Don't call him. Don't answer his calls. Don't
let him come over. Don't meet him for breakfast, lunch, or dinner. Don't let him give you money. Don't let him buy you anything to get back in. Let him go, so you can move on. You don't
have to explain why you've moved on, he'll figure it out. Forget
about wanting closure.

On the other hand, we get letters like this one, where a

woman is just completely oblivious to the level of stupidity she's involved in:

Subject: In Love with a Momma's Boy!!!

I'm a 22-year-old mother of two who's deeply in love with a momma's boy. We recently split from our three-and-a-half year relationship. He brought not only the police to my house—and you're not going to believe this—but his mom as well to get his things. I feel like his mom came along because she knows if he would've come alone we would have made up. The argument that set in motion the end of our relationship happened because he left for one destination yet somehow ended up at the club.

Without so much as a phone call, he strolled up in here at four A.M. My thing is, "Fine, you decided to go to the club, but have respect for me and call." So when he came home I told him to leave. I meant, "Let me cool down, you cool down, and we'll talk about this later!" The following day when he brought the goon (his mom) with him, they not only gathered his clothes, but also things that weren't his— tissues, paper towels, an area rug, trash can, trash bags. He even had my cell phone disconnected and did other petty things of that nature! He did all this in the presence of the kids.

The whole time they were crying, screaming "Daddy," and he was whisking past them like they weren't there! I feel that his actions were done out of spite, but what reason does he have to be upset? Even if he found some stupid reason, the kids didn't have anything to do with it. My question to you all is: Am I wrong for not wanting him in our lives because of his immaturity, but also because he keeps his mom in

our business, and he seems to be easily persuaded? I will not lie, I do
love this man, and I do miss him, and the kids love him as well, but
his being spiteful and just plain stupid is a whole other story!

What this woman is talking about is mind-blowing. She's
young and she has to know that the worst part about her situation is that their kids do not have their father in the home. But
this momma's boy should've never been in the home in the
first place.

Seriously, what man brings his momma to the house to help
him pack? Yeah, he's a momma's boy all right, and she's better
off without him. Obviously he's not ready to be a man, and
she's way more mature at 22 than he'll ever be. But she's not
using common sense. She's being stupid!

I go back to the countless hours I spent with Steve reading
drafts, listening to his thoughts, and even offering insight from
my experiences as he completed each of his books. I really saw
the light when he wrote *Act Like a Lady, Think Like a Man.* It
sparked a major epiphany, opening my eyes as to why men
think and do the things they do. Things I never knew before;
like why men cheat, lie, don't keep commitments. So, when
we don't lay out the requirements of what we need in a relationship, or share with men our standards and goals, we suffer
in the game of love.

I realized that it's time for women to take responsibility for
our actions in our relationships and stop being stupid. Understand, when I say "stupid" I say it with love, but tough love. So
often we simply don't take time to think our choices or actions
through.

How many times have we gone into relationships led by our

emotions and not our brain? Then when the relationship goes bad we sit back and blame the other party. Or we get into relationships because we're desperate. Maybe our friends are in relationships, and we want what they have. We want it so much that we hook up with a person who may not be the best for us.

We ignore red flags and warning signs that are clearly there. We even ignore it when the man has another woman. But women need to think about how a lot of these relationships start. It took me years to finally figure out what I had been doing wrong in relationships. I thought I had it all together, being an attractive woman, with a good job, my own car, good credit, good friends, and a man! But something was missing. Frankly, looks, money, and material things alone don't bring happiness or guarantee a healthy, successful relationship. If we don't take the time to make a self-assessment and look back at our situation then we're destined to repeat those exact mistakes. But hey, it's not when you learn the lesson, it's that you learn the lesson before you die, and learning is an ongoing process.

I opened this book writing about taking inventory, because I want us to start looking at our lives, taking review of ourselves, and working from the inside out. Ask yourself these questions: What kind of relationship do I want? Why am I not in this type of relationship? What were the problems in my last one? Why do I keep making the same mistakes? But you can stop this by changing your behavior, getting off automatic pilot, and paying attention to your life, right here, right now. The woman in this letter really needs to hear me loud and clear!

We have to analyze what happened the last time we were involved with someone. It's not just his fault the relationship didn't work. We've heard this a bazillion times, but a man can only do to us what we allow. Ask yourself, why are you allowing these same things to happen time and time again? What is it about you that attracts the same type of individuals? It's not him, it's you.

Look at people whose relationships you don't like. You could probably tell that woman a hundred reasons you wouldn't be in that particular situation and what she should or shouldn't do, and what you would or wouldn't take, etc. But if you're in the thick of it, you may not be able to see it when it's happening to you—even if people around you are telling you to move on because he's no good.

You don't have to be stupid all your life. Get out. You can change the situation right now! You gotta want to change, but first you gotta know that you need changing.

Strawberry Tip:

De-Nile is a river in Egypt,

so get out of denial!

CHAPTER FIVE

Bad Boys, Bad Boys, Whatcha Gonna Do?

SUBJECT: *Troubled Relationship*

I have been in a relationship with my boyfriend for three years now. Recently, we had a very big argument about him flirting with another woman and he ended up choking me after I poured a bucket of water on him and called him all the names in the world. The police were involved and now he is asking me to drop the case against him and give him another chance. He is undergoing counseling and I am really confused about whether I should stay with him or leave. Please advise.

It's amazing how you can see yourself one way while others perceive you in a totally different manner. People see you at work as a strong, independent, smart woman who's in charge and all that. But at home you're this helpless little coward afraid to speak up, afraid to have an opinion, afraid to make the wrong move. You're afraid to speak too loudly, and you tiptoe around because you're afraid you might upset him and "make" him hit you. You even make excuses for the bruises that you have on your body and your face.

You walk around in such a haze and a fog and in such a stupor that you believe him when he says he's not going to hit you anymore. You constantly try not to upset him, because you don't want to hurt *him* and make him feel badly. You care way more about him than you do about yourself. And when he does hit you again, because he will, he says, "Why did you make me do this?"

Reading the letter at the beginning of this chapter was difficult for me because it brought back a lot of painful and disturbing memories. Things I've never discussed publicly before now.

As a young woman I had very low self-esteem. I was young—19—and the man I got involved with and eventually lived with was horribly abusive. He was a monster who beat me for kicks and giggles. Simply because he could. I have scars on my body to this day from those beatings.

I let him talk to me disrespectfully and treat me as if I were his personal property. He would walk all over me, cheat on me, take my money. And no matter what I did to please him, it was never good enough. For a while, I thought this was my life, and that this was how relationships were supposed to be. I saw no way out. I think part of my acceptance of how he treated me, or should I say *mis*treated me, came from me simply not knowing what to do. I was terrified of him.

They say time heals. It has, because I can talk about it now. I might be on an episode of *Snapped* if he tried to do that to me today. But back then . . . I guess I can chalk it up to immaturity, low self-esteem, and lack of knowledge. Too bad "The Strawberry Letter" wasn't around at that time.

I stayed with him way too long. We were both from the Midwest and had both moved down south, where I got a job as the news director at a radio station.

Looking back, I gave him my power and he totally took advantage of me once he saw I would never challenge anything he did. I treated him like a king. He went on to become a tyrant and a dictator.

My breaking point came one morning as I was getting dressed for work. He busted me in my eye. I don't remember what we were arguing about; probably nothing, because it was never about anything major. He had beat me before, but this time he made me late for work, and that was a first. He knew how important my job was. I decided right then and there that it was time for me to get out.

In hindsight, I think he had developed a great deal of jealousy toward me. I was getting better at my job, moving up, and becoming more popular. He didn't like all the attention I was receiving. He was losing control of his little puppet: me.

My co-workers would see him acting a fool in the mornings when he dropped me off for work. We'd be parked in front of the station arguing in the car. Sometimes they might see me with a black eye or a bruise.

I finally confided in some of them, and they helped me to see that something—no, everything—about him and that relationship was wrong.

My co-workers would invite me to their homes or to lunch and provided much-needed shoulders to cry on. Through our conversations I began to see myself and my life differently. There was a light at the end of the tunnel of my personal purgatory. Thank God I started opening up about what was going on. So, I say to women, talk to people. I don't care how ashamed or embarrassed you may feel. The sooner you talk about the abuse, the quicker your life can change for the better.

You have to find someone you trust and take that mask off. Let people know what is going on, because they might be in a position to help you. There are things you can't deal with by yourself. If I had stayed with him I'd probably be dead by now.

I'll never forget the day I finally made up my mind to leave him. I was 27 by then and had decided enough was enough. I bought a plane ticket to go back to Chicago. I didn't have a job waiting there for me, but I had my family. That was all that mattered. I was getting out. I still thank God to this day that I opened my mouth, because breaking the silence and telling people around me what was happening was how I got free. My co-workers helped me plan my escape.

One of the big responsibilities I had as news director was to write the quarterly reports. I hated doing them and I'd always wait until the last minute to turn them in. However, those quarterly reports may have saved my life.

The night before my deadline I stayed at work really late working on them. I remember calling him from work. He commented in a suspicious tone, "Wow, you must really have a lot to do." I nervously replied, "Yeah, quarterly reports, you know how that is, but I gotta get them done." What he didn't know was that I was desperate to get all the reports done so I could get out of town.

I didn't want to leave anything for anyone else at the station to have to clean up. They had already done so much for me. I was uncertain and terrified about the future. I didn't know when or even if I was ever coming back. But I was on a mission. I got home and laid my clothes out for the next day, and the morning couldn't come fast enough. I didn't sleep well that night.

I got up around four-thirty the next morning, got dressed, and tiptoed out of the bedroom. The week prior, I started taking garments out of my closet a little at a time, stuffing them daily into my work bag. I had been careful not to take too much so he wouldn't notice. My bag was already packed and in my co-worker's car. He was waiting outside for me. My heart was pounding so hard I thought it would come through my chest, and just as I was about to walk out the door, he woke up. My heart stopped and I was frozen with fear as he groggily called out, "Boy, you're up early."

Suddenly my adrenaline kicked in and, thinking fast on my feet, I replied, "Yeah, you know those quarterlies." I was worried he was going to wake up fully and see that my clothes weren't in the closet and put two and two together. The slightest clue could've given it all away. He got up and I went back into the bedroom to kiss him good-bye so he wouldn't suspect anything. That seemed to satisfy him, and after that I wasted no time getting out of there.

I raced out the door, hopped in my friend's car, and he drove me to the airport. I never looked back. I don't think I exhaled until I saw the signs for the airport. The thought that one slip in the plan would've been a total disaster is still chilling. That was the last I saw of the co-worker who took me to the airport, but I will be forever grateful to him.

I felt relief when the plane touched down in Chicago, despite the fact that I didn't have a job. I didn't know what I was going to do, but it didn't matter. I just knew I had to get away from the hell I had been living in. For some reason, I never feared or thought that he'd follow me or try to come looking for me.

I didn't tell anyone back home what had happened, and during my time down south, only told my mom minor details of the problems I was having. But a mother knows. I remember she would always say, "Well, when you get tired you'll leave." That day had finally come.

Yes, I had finally gotten tired and left. Eventually, I confessed to my mom about the abuse, and when my brother found out I had to talk him out of going down to Texas and putting a hurting on that man. My brother was just being protective, but for me, at that point, it was over and done. I had to go about the process of healing.

Oh, that man definitely tested me. I knew he wasn't going to give up that easily. He called several times, harassing me. Fortunately, it stopped rather quickly, because no one bought into his lies. He told my mother I was cheating on him, and that I was deranged and on drugs and needed to be institutionalized. He said anything he thought could make me look bad in her eyes. My brother is really the one who shut all that calling stuff down. Cowards can't handle a real man.

Two years later I saw him. I was working at a local radio

station in Chicago, and we were out at a park doing an event. He actually walked up to me and hugged me. I could feel him trembling. He hugged me for a long time, until finally I had to tell him to let go and I backed away. At that time forgiveness was the furthest thing from my mind, but I had definitely moved on with my life.

He called me again after our brief encounter, but I wasn't very nice. I told him everything he did and that he needed to take responsibility for his actions. He was in denial and told me that it had all been my fault. It was pitiful to hear him lying to himself. Honestly, it made me feel more empowered. It felt good to finally stand up to this sick man. I later found out that he had witnessed abusive behavior growing up.

When I look back at that time in my life, those turbulent eight years, I realize I never thought about marrying him. I guess I instinctively knew he wasn't the one for me.

After that I experienced a string of bad relationships, but nothing like that one. One time I got into a pretty bad physical fight with a guy I was dating, but I fought back. I had made up my mind that I was never going to let another man abuse me like that. It was like the scene in the movie *What's Love Got to Do With It,* when Tina finally fought back. Yeah, that was me!

My message to women:

First of all, don't keep it all in. If you can get out, then get out. Realize it's not your fault. No one deserves abuse, but you have to wake up and open your eyes. Ask yourself these questions: Why do you want to be in a relationship where someone is beating you? What about that kind of behavior says "I love you"? Do you really know what love is? Do you love yourself?

If you know what love truly is you will not tolerate an abusive relationship. Understand, I'm not talking about him loving you, or you loving him. I'm talking about you loving yourself enough to know when something isn't working. There is no love involved in a situation where a man is beating you down verbally or physically. It's about him exerting control over you.

Oh, that man had me going to see a therapist and everything. He would always tell me, "You need to go to a psychiatrist. You're crazy!" One day I took him up on it. I went to see a psychologist, who said, point blank, "I don't see a thing wrong with you based on what you've told me. It's really him!"

When I got home he asked what she'd told me, and I said, "She thought you were crazy and that I was in a crazy relationship!" He was furious and ordered me never to go back to that person and to go see someone else. That was my first realization that it wasn't me. I was okay and nothing was wrong with me other than having low self-esteem.

The moral of this story is that we as women can't be afraid to tell someone—our mothers, our fathers, our pastors, our friends, an uncle—when we are in unhealthy relationships. If you can't talk about it, write about it in your journal and let someone read it. And if you're too scared to do that, do some research online. Check out abuse and where it starts. Learn about support groups. Also make a decision not to be a victim anymore.

If you stay in an abusive relationship, I truly believe that something will die. Either you'll die physically or spiritually. Don't keep it bottled up! Back then I didn't have the relationship with God that I do now. But I will say, going through that horrible situation helped lead me closer to God. It was unfortunate it had to happen in order for my spiritual life to get right, but the end result of getting closer to God is most important.

I'm not an angel and I'm not perfect. At that time if I'd had a close relationship with God I know I would not have stayed with that man, and definitely not for eight years. It's not easy for me to come clean about it even now. However, I don't mind sharing, because I'm free of that situation. Thank you, God. You can be free too. You can get out of it.

Strawberry Tip

If God blesses you with another day, then it's another chance to make things right.

CHAPTER SIX

What a Girl Wants

SUBJECT: Go with Love or Go with Money

I'm an attractive single female, 37 years old, with a great personality, good job. I've never married and have no children. After the loss of my father I took myself out of the dating game for a while for a period of healing. Recently someone from my past reappeared and we have been spending some great quality time together and I'm really falling for him. And then another "blast from the past" shows up who is now professing his love for me. I like them both but am having a problem deciding which one to choose. The first one is tall, handsome, has a great sense of humor, is smart, and we have great chemistry. However, he's been married a few times and really can't do anything for me financially. The other man is tall, handsome, has a great sense of humor, and is smart. The chemistry is there but not as strong as with the first man, although he is financially set, has a beautiful home, and can provide for me. My heart wants to go with man number one but my heart has led me astray before and I wonder if I should go with the one who can provide for me? I just need someone else's point of view right now! Thank you.

Ahh, the toils and trials of dating! Shaking the past is tough. When I weigh everything I've been through, I think, is it really going to be worth it getting to know this other person? Then I run for the hills. To be brutally honest, I flat-out hate dating, and reading this letter reminds me of why! There's always this mental tug and pull of do I go with this guy, because of such and such, or that guy, because of so and so. Then of course you have the dreaded scenario of not being able to meet a good guy, so you begin to wonder what's wrong with you!

I wish we could just skip the whole dating "thing" and get right to the marriage part. I think I have subconsciously put myself in a *non*-dating rut as a result of my frustration. Sometimes I wonder if I'll ever remarry! Of course I have hope. Unfortunately, the women in my family have frightening track records when it comes to marriage, so that's not very encouraging.

This all may sound completely crazy, given the fact that I give advice to millions daily, but I've never had a good relationship with a man.

Think about it. If you're like me, you may have put the kind of guy that you want, or that you would like to have, so far into the stratosphere in terms of expectations, subconsciously you know you'll never find that person. So no one will satisfy you or measure up to that ideal.

Guys give me their numbers all the time. I have a number right now that I've been holding on to all week, and this guy's cute, has a good job, but something is stopping me from calling. What if I have in my hand the number of the man who could be "the one"? I may never know, because my fear of failure is so paralyzing that I'd rather just not even try. Many of my friends are frustrated with me for this exact reason.

Ask any of them. They'll tell you that any guy who meets me loves me. They think I'm attractive, I have a sparkling personality, the total package. One-on-one on a date, I'm fun. We laugh, we talk, but after that I may not want to ever see him or talk to him again, and that's fine with me. There's something wrong with that, I know.

For some reason, after the introductions I shut down. I start doubting myself and the insecurities set in. Do you ever feel that way? I think it's some kind of getting-to-know-a-new-person phobia! I'm the first to tell you that if you fall off the horse, get back on. I guess I need to take my own advice, huh?

Everyone is always trying to hook me up and take me out to meet guys. My co-worker Carla Ferrell is so done with me. She's gotten on the air, even getting Tommy and Steve to chime in, and they put me on blast, saying, "You can give her your number, but she ain't gonna call you back! Something's wrong with that!"

Recently, I came across a little paragraph in a magazine that said: "Are you too single?" And I wondered what that meant. Could I be just too single? It's not like I don't want a mate, but I'm used to being on my own.

Maybe it's just not my time. A male friend once told me,

"Shirley, God is preparing your man for you, and because you're so special it's taking a little longer."

I truly believe in my heart the right kind of love with the *right* man will happen in my life. There's just no reason why it shouldn't! I have to keep my faith strong. And everybody just needs to back up off me, instead of judging the fact that I'm single! There are worse things in life.

I mean, really, ladies, where is it written that there's a timetable? That you have to have a man by a certain age or else? I understand the pressure to get married as women get older—we want to have a family, and we have our biological clocks to consider. But Lord in heaven knows I'm not having any more children. I don't even know if I *can* have any more children. On second thought, I don't want the answer to that question.

My girlfriends have accused me of being too picky. For the record, I don't agree. I just want what I want.

1. He must believe in God.
2. He cannot be insecure or controlling!
3. He must have some sort of legitimate financial means.
4. He must be a gentleman (you know, the basics, like opening doors).
5. He must *love* women.

Okay, can we just talk about that last one for a minute? He's got to love women! Not in that playa-mentality kind of way. No, he needs to love women in the sense that he can't live without them. He wants them by his side.

He loves their company, the way they smell, talk, walk. He can appreciate the beauty, but when your head is turned he's not trying to reach over and get another woman's number. And I don't want an insecure, crazy man. No way!

Oh, and I'd like him to be tall and handsome. When I say "handsome," I mean I want him to have good grooming, nice teeth, dress well, be clean, and of course smell good!

That said, having a checklist is *not*—I repeat, *not*—being picky. If you have a checklist, more power to you. I say, have it in your mind, but don't engrave it in stone. You know what I mean. The ones that say: he has to make X dollars; he has to drive X kind of car; he has to be no shorter than 5'11" and no taller than 6'6". Let's be realistic!

Lately, with all the "cougar" talk, I've even been asked if I would ever date a younger guy. Sure I would! But I absolutely don't consider myself a cougar. To me, that term denotes predatory tendencies. I'm certainly not out there on the prowl for younger men. Although, that seems to be what I attract, and I don't see anything wrong with it. They just need to be mature in their thinking and have themselves together.

The men my age want younger women. But in all fairness, there are some great "older-younger" guys. You know, men who are older with young spirits. I like to consider myself a great older-younger woman! Maybe that will explain my strange fixation with Morgan Freeman.

Okay, so there, I announced it to the world: Morgan Freeman is Shirley Strawberry's crush! He's the ideal older-younger man, I think. He's actually the only older man that I really like. Now, come on, the chances of Morgan Freeman and me hooking up are one in a zillion, but I love him. He's tall and seems like the perfect Southern gentleman.

Ooh, I don't know, after that accident he was in. The tabloids reported that he was with his wife's best friend. But anyway, he hurt his hand in that accident, and I would've loved nursing him back to health! I'll never get him, and if I did, oh my God, I'd probably run.

Tommy, Steve, and Carla tease me on the show all the time. Tommy does a great impersonation from *Shawshank Redemption* when Morgan Freeman, in that deep, robust, sexy, and refined voice, says, "Me and Andy Dufresne!" Or from *Lean on Me* when Morgan says, "Get them chains off the door! The enemy is here!"

Then everyone laughs, so I guess that's the closest I'll get to him other than watching all his movies over and over and over again. Besides, didn't he just marry or try to marry his step-granddaughter? Maybe I should rethink my crush.

It's tricky out here looking for love, and it's more complicated if you're a single mother trying to date.

I'm in a scary place right now. Many of you may be, too. But what I do know is that we can't open up to the future if we're holding on to the past—past pain, past regrets, past mistakes. I have to give it to the woman in the letter. At least she's out there actively dating. I can identify with her, because she had her mind made up until another "blast from the past" resurfaced. Boy, have I been there.

I say, timing is everything in life and in relationships. It's the past for a reason, and what we can't allow ourselves to do is lament over a what-coulda-been. I'm not going to lie, to this day a tiny smile creeps across my face when I think about the one who maybe got away, because there was a place in the back of my mind and heart that kept the door open to him for a long time.

His name was Michael and we met while I was working in Chicago. Since I was in radio and he was in the record business it made for a natural connection. We dated for several years, and in my heart I really wanted the relationship to develop into something more serious.

But he made it clear that marriage wasn't in the cards because of the failure of his own parents' marriage. I took him at his word and dismissed the idea of marrying him, even though that's what I wanted. After I got a job offer in California and moved to Los Angeles, we would have fun during his visits, but I don't think we communicated like we should have.

We never got down to the real business of our relationship: what I wanted, whether or not he'd be willing to change his attitude about marriage (he was not a fan). It never seemed to be the right time. You know we can always use that excuse when we're trying to avoid something. While he would always fly to see me, I never returned the favor, which upset him and caused him to tell me that I never put any effort into the relationship. But why should I? He said he didn't want to marry me.

Eventually, the relationship ended, and even though I kept in touch with him and the love was still there, I continued living my life in Los Angeles. I soon met and started dating another Michael (I must have a thing for Michaels), whom I would eventually marry (and divorce, but more about that later).

The grown-up decent thing for me to do was to let Michael back in Chicago know I was getting married. After all, we had agreed to keep the lines of communication open. But before I could, he found out through a mutual friend, and he was devastated.

Years later, after I separated from my husband and I was somewhat single again, preparing to go through a divorce, we tried to get back together. But he had been so hurt before that he could never fully trust me with his heart again. He moved on with his life and started dating someone else, but they haven't married either.

In the end, I think we both really loved each other, but I suppose neither of us knew how to close the deal. We're still friends, but we'll never get together.

Maybe if I had just told him what I wanted. Hmmmm . . .

I'll chalk it up to what Ms. Badu sang: "I guess I'll see you next lifetime . . ."

Strawberry Tip:

Know what you want, say what you want,

and get what you want!

CHAPTER SEVEN

Lashes, Lipstick, & Stilettos

SUBJECT: Thirty-second Man

I am currently in a relationship with a gentleman who brings me flowers just because, runs my bathwater, gives me back rubs and foot rubs. So what's the problem, you ask? Well, the bedroom. He's a thirty-second man. No exaggeration! This is extremely frustrating to me because previously I had been in a six-year relationship with a thug who cracked my back, had me calling out Mary, Jesus, and Joseph, and calling him Big Daddy as I experienced La Petite Morte every time we were intimate.

The problem with that relationship was the way he treated me outside of the bedroom. He would cheat, flirt in front of me, and lie. So, I decided I needed to be treated well at all times, not just in the bedroom. I left my thug for this gentleman. I am not one to cheat, but Lord, a girl is frustrated. Some advice please, before I lose my mind.

Don't kick a man out the bedroom because he isn't satisfying you sexually if everything else in the relationship is working. I'm sure it's frustrating, but it's a problem that *can* be fixed, barring him suffering from any sort of medical condition.

I do commend the woman in the letter for getting away from the thug and realizing that she deserved better, but now she needs to open her mouth and say what she wants and teach her new man how to love her.

I work next to a really strong man, and Steve talks about how women set the tone for the relationships we get into. We know this, ladies, that's why we've got to not only *say* what we want, but *lay out* what we want and need. As women we have to step up and talk to our men, and teach them about what we like and don't like.

Get that man on track and I'm sure you can turn around the intimacy problems and have a lovely relationship. You have to be patient and take some bad with the good as you work through things. Getting to know our bodies may not always be easy for us, let alone the man we are dating, but if that man and the relationship really mean a lot to you, you must put the effort in, and things will get better and even out.

I think that if this woman approached the "good guy" in a delicate way, because these things are sensitive, she would be successful and have the total package. A lot of times it's not what we do, it's *how* we do it. This is a *good* guy. I mean, who in this day and age runs bathwater for his woman?

I have to be frank, that's a very rare situation. I'm not saying the guys who don't are bad guys. I love them, too, but this woman has a diamond here. She has a gem and she needs to appreciate him. Women always talk about what we want in a man, but when we get what we want, we sometimes don't know how to act!

So ladies, while we're making the demands for our men to "deliver" in the bedroom, and just on the romantic tip in general, remember to do your part to keep it sexy! Romance is a two-way street. And don't stop your efforts when you get him. We play just as big a part in keeping the "magic" and passion alive throughout the relationship.

Now, here's the really crazy part. I go out of my house every day looking nice for a reason, and let me tell you, it's not just for myself. In the back of my mind I'm hoping that I meet someone. I want to look good, wear sexy shoes, put on my lipstick and my lashes! I may be terrified to date, but I *do* consider those our secret weapon, ladies. They are what I consider the essence of a woman. Seriously, they are our armor, our uniform even.

When we're dressed up and wearing our lashes (my preferred beauty accessory), lipstick, and stilettos, we feel beautiful and womanly. Of course, there's more to a woman than this, but they help define us. And lipstick, lashes, and stilettos can get you into anywhere. They can even get you into church! No one's going to turn you down.

But please, to this woman or anyone else whose back has been "cracked" by a thug, don't go back to the thug just for some sexual thrills and lose out on a really good man. Just reach into your bag of tricks. Don't toss him out, talk it out!

Strawberry Tip:

Lashes, lipstick, and stilettos can cure a

multitude of sins and get you just

about anything you want!

CHAPTER EIGHT

Yours, Mine, Ours

SUBJECT: Whose House Is It?

My husband allows his 16-year-old son to have sex with teenage girls in our house. We have been married for five years and my husband owned the house we live in before we got married. He told me that since my name is not on the deed I cannot disagree with him concerning matters that occur within our house. He also said that if I don't like his son having sex in the house that I can get out and purchase my own home because he can manage without me. Steve and Shirley, is this a sign that my husband is ready to move on without me? Should I file for divorce? I no longer feel important or needed by him. What should I do?

L adies: women are to be cherished and respected. If the men in our lives can't do that, then what on earth are we doing with them? Your wife is supposed to be someone you can love and honor, someone you want to protect. So why would you want to treat her any other kind of way *but* that!

And to all *real* men who are doing that on the regular: Much love and keep up the good work!

When I read this letter I felt her pain deep down, but it also infuriated me, for two reasons. First, because if your husband loves you like a husband should, he would never say such horrible things. No husband should speak to his wife like this man did. Second, because this woman clearly allowed him to do so before and after marriage, so I'm not surprised at what he said. She never realized or asserted her power with this man.

She needs to sit back and assess her life thus far, and any woman reading this book who may be putting up with this type of mess from her husband or boyfriend needs to do the same.

Where's the love here? This is about material things and "what's mine is mine." There is nothing that says *ours* in this relationship. Look, I don't care if your name is on the deed or not, if you're married to that person, it's half your house, period. Remember in the movie *Diary of a Mad Black Woman* when Madea had the buzz saw and she was going to cut the furniture in half? You get the picture.

And you *know* that it is wrong for a 16-year-old kid to be having sex in his parents' house, and not only is it wrong, it's disrespectful. I'm sure the writer of this letter has been contributing to that house in ways that, if you could put a dollar amount on it, would be much more than the monthly mortgage. Tally up the cooking, cleaning, taking care of the kids, working a job, etc. Cha-ching! You'd be filthy rich.

This woman needs to have a serious conversation with her husband and speak her mind just like she did in the letter, and be confident and firm. This is not the time to be a punk. If he's disagreeable or doesn't try to meet her halfway, then maybe he isn't the man for her.

As far as men talking to women crazy, if there's any hint of it from the very beginning, we need to check 'em! Stop that man right then and there! Don't wait to do it because you think he'll change later. It's about asserting yourself and saying, "Excuse me, I wish you wouldn't talk to me like that" or "I can't allow you to speak to me in those terms." Thank you! Amen!

What this all boils down to is that women are notorious for staying in relationships way past the expiration date. I myself have done it. For instance, I stayed in my marriage way longer than I should have. I knew that it wasn't going to work pretty much on our honeymoon, but I wanted my marriage to succeed. I wanted the marriage. I guess I had too much pride to just give up. I didn't want to be a quitter.

I thought in my mind that God would restore my relationship with my husband if I prayed hard enough, all the time not realizing that it just wasn't the right fit for me. I think I knew deep down that I shouldn't have married Michael, but did it anyway.

He was a nice guy, but not marriage material at the time. I thought love could conquer all and that I could love this man enough to make him love me the way I needed to be loved. Wrong! Remember, ladies, just because you're there and ready doesn't mean that man is. The best thing I could've done was let go.

A man who speaks badly to a woman clearly has some insecurities and control issues. There has to be something in the way that man was brought up. Maybe it was what he learned in the streets or from some guys with that "pimp" mentality. Marriage is a partnership, a love and commitment partnership, and both parties should be respected and heard!

Strawberry Tip:

Let that man know in no uncertain terms, if we can't treat each other with love and respect, you *can* and *will* move on!

CHAPTER NINE

Clean Up Your Act

SUBJECT: My Wife and Drugs

I have been with my wife for four years and I love her with all my heart and soul. She has five children; none are mine biologically, but I love them like they are. But my wife has a "problem" with cocaine and it is destroying our relationship. She hangs around drug users and dealers and considers them her friends and says that I don't understand her like they do. She has lost her kids to family services 'cause she would not go to any of the treatment programs they provided for her. She does not work and barely takes care of the house. My wife says I don't love her even though I am still with her because I believe she will do better. She told me one of the reasons she uses cocaine is so she will not cheat on me. That just crushed me. I love her with all my heart and soul, but we are not going anywhere and I want

better not just for me but for both of us. I don't know if I should just
give up or try to fight it out.

It's been four years and his wife's "problem" is not getting any better, it's getting worse. One thing's for sure, you can't make a person quit an addiction if she's in denial. I learned that from one of my closest girlfriends, who was addicted to crack for eighteen years! We met when she was in her late thirties, after she had gotten clean. She is now in her forties, and to see her today you'd never know the hell she's been through.

Her skin and hair are beautiful. Her eyes are bright! I feel her triumph each time I see her. It's amazing how resilient the human spirit and mind are. I know everybody hasn't had such a victory in their lives from being in the deep depths of drug abuse. But the mind is powerful. If we really want something we can achieve it.

My girlfriend has a very optimistic and positive outlook on life now, and that crack addict is just another person in her past. If she looks back it's only to remind herself of how strong she is or to tell you her story. She is living proof that you can overcome the worst in life.

The man in the letter says he loves his wife with all his heart. Well, sometimes love means walking away. Sometimes love means loving yourself enough to know that you deserve better. Of course, only you can decide that.

What I can conclude from this letter is that if anyone reading this book has found himself in the same or similar situation, and you've tried to get your loved one in some kind of treatment program and it didn't work, then don't let the person pull you down along with him. It's like being married to someone who is married to drugs.

Basically, this man has some decisions to make. He should try again to get his wife in rehab. But I think drugs are enough of a reason to walk away.

Sometimes marriages just don't work for whatever reason— and believe me drugs are a great reason. I used to work in radio with a guy who was an addict. He would free-base. I didn't know what was going on. I knew he was missing an awful lot of days at work. I did the seven P.M. to midnight shift and he came on after me, and there were so many times that I had to stay late and cover for him. I'd get no phone call, no notice that he was taking off, no nothing.

When the clock struck twelve I would be ready to go, purse in hand. Back then, before everything was automated, we would have to pull the music for the next jock for the first hour of his or her show. So by the time my shift was over I'd have his music pulled, would have played all his commercials, and he still wouldn't have showed up.

Finally, a couple of hours into his show, he'd eventually get to work, but he offered no explanation for his lateness. He'd come in like nothing happened, with a "Hey, Shirley, how ya doin'? What's happening?" *Hey, Shirley, how you doin'? What? I just worked two, almost three hours overtime for you, and that's it? Hey, Shirley, how you doin? Man, please!*

One day I confronted him. "Hey, what's happening? Why are you missing so many days, coming in late all the time? What's going on with you?" And he sat me down and told me exactly what was going on with him. It was way more than I'd bargained for.

I was shocked and devastated. I didn't know anything about free-basing, but I knew after hearing his story that I would never ever get involved with it. I couldn't afford to have something make me miss work or mess up with my family. I was just his co-worker. He was married with children. Imagine how horrible it was to be his wife, or the damage his addiction was doing to his kids. He was a very smart guy, well educated, but he got caught up. He was able to function and work, but there were times that he would be so wiped out, he didn't care about anything else but his high.

You cannot make a person get off drugs if he's not ready. Sometimes you need to enlist other people and do an intervention. However, after you've given it all you've got and you can't do anything else, you've got to know when to fold 'em and get out! I hate to say this, because I strongly believe in marriage, but drugs and marriage don't go together, like black stockings and white shoes!

This is such a tough subject that I couldn't just talk about *one* of the letters Steve and I received. I had to include this next one.

Subject: My Mom Keeps on Drinking and It's Getting a Little Hard for Me to Handle

My mom likes to celebrate my birthdays. She's fun and cool but she also scares me because every time she drinks she gets drunk. She yells, hits, and breaks stuff. Even at the parties that aren't mine. It's embarrassing and sad. I just wish that there could be one party where she wouldn't do that. I want to take her to a doctor, but she doesn't want to get help. And then the next day she doesn't remember what happened. Please help me. My birthday is coming up and I don't want the same thing to happen again.

When I read this letter, I was just so sorry that this girl had to go through what she went through. She's young and should be enjoying her life, preparing for her future, and hanging out with her friends. Instead, she has a terrible burden that she has to deal with at home.

She loves her mother very much and doesn't want to call the police on her. But quite frankly, her mother is out of control and needs some help. Sometimes if our parents are in denial and they don't want to get help, we have to get help for ourselves, such as from Al-Anon or Alateen (for younger members), or by asking other family members for their support. Statistics say that each alcoholic affects the lives of at least four other people in your family, and what is described above is a prime example.

This young woman may have to go as far as recording her mother on video, allowing her to see how awful and embarrassingly she acts when she's drunk. Maybe that will be enough to snap her out of it. But if it isn't, this young lady needs to save herself and get some professional assistance. Hopefully, there's someone in her life she can reach out to for help.

Maybe you think, *Man, if this person sees how much I love her, she'll stop.* Or maybe you think that you can love the person enough to *make* her give up her particular addiction.

But it doesn't work like that. All you end up doing is enabling the person, and maybe giving her a pass and a pardon to do it whenever she wants to. It will get to a point where she won't even bother hiding her addiction anymore, because she'll think what she's doing is okay. That's why enabling isn't the answer. Tough love is. Get her some help!

Do the research, get in the Yellow Pages, search the Internet. Sometimes churches have outreach programs. Do what you can to see that the person gets help, by any means necessary.

You can't allow yourself to be afraid to change your situation. I know it's scary, because you wonder, What if I let go and I don't have anyone else and then I'll be alone? That fear of being alone makes us stay in bad situations, and tolerate and accept things that we shouldn't.

We may call it love, but it's not. It's really the fear of what's on the other side. But I guarantee what's on that side is an opportunity to open yourself up to the *real* love you deserve!

Strawberry Tip:

Get help or get out! Pick one!

CHAPTER TEN

What Did You Say?

SUBJECT: *Deeply in Love but Hurting Inside*

I have been married to my husband for thirteen years and throughout my marriage I have been faithful. My husband put me in a situation that disturbs me to my core. My husband told me one night that we were going dancing. Since he never takes me out I jumped at the offer. We had to stop at his friend's house to pick up him and his girlfriend because we were going on a double date.

His friend's girlfriend was running late so my husband's friend stepped outside to call her. My husband started groping me. I felt uncomfortable, but he wanted me to be spontaneous so I went with it. We proceeded to his friend's bedroom. We heard the friend's front door open so my husband called out to make sure it was his friend and not a stranger walking in his house. Before I knew it the friend walked in the room pulling off his shirt. My husband told me he was

about to make my fantasy come true. WHAT THE HECK!! All I could
do was scream and run.

I asked what he was thinking. He said we discussed this scenario
in the heat of passion. In the heat of passion who knows what the
heck I said? Now he wants us to go to counseling but I don't think so.
I suspect he has done this before. I'm so hurt and disgusted and I can
never look at him the same. I am a Christian woman but know how
to satisfy him . . . or so I thought. I'm leaning toward leaving my
marriage and never returning. Please steer me in the right direction.

You know, we've probably all heard the phrase "I lost my-self in you" or "I don't know who I am anymore." That simply means that you put yourself last in the relationship. You put the other person's needs before your own, and you con-sider what he wants before you voice your opinion of what you want to do.

Ladies, let's remember that when we're in a relationship, we still have to be ourselves. It's a beautiful thing if you have a mate who is supportive of you being yourself. I've made the mistake in the past of losing myself in a man so I know how the woman in the letter feels.

This woman's husband is way out of order, but she's clearly lost her voice in the relationship and needs to find it immedi-ately. Who wants to be with a doormat, someone with no opinion, and quite frankly someone who's not a challenge any-more? Now the man is searching for someone who gives him the thrill he needs, since she's allowed him to push her down and walk all over her.

Don't get me wrong, there's nothing bad about being sup-portive or making sure the other person is taken care of, but not to the point that you neglect yourself or you don't know who you are anymore when you look in the mirror. You value everything that comes out of his mouth, and everything he does, placing little value on what you have to offer. That is certainly no way to live. I guarantee your partner is not going to be feeling you too much after you've gone into doormat status.

It could set the relationship up for a lot of things, like cheating, because you're no longer the woman that man used to respect and love. You've even lost sight of your goals and dreams. It's very important to stay who you are. That doesn't mean that you don't make adjustments and compromises for the betterment of the relationship. Just be careful not to give up your self-respect in the process.

When I look back at my marriage, I definitely lost myself, probably before we got to the altar. I think outward pressure, society, family, age—all those things factored into my thinking at the time. I wanted to get married and when I saw my exhusband, Michael, I was attracted to him, and that's really all it was. So much more should have been considered before we decided to marry.

I met him at church. He was even a deacon! He seemed like a nice enough guy. I was sold! On our first date we talked about marriage, children, and everything else under the sun. And from that day forward my goal was to marry him. He had a great last name and in my head I'd already put our names together: SHIRLEY STRAWBERRY. Have you ever done that?

I jumped into dating this man with both feet, and not long after that he asked me to marry him.

Truthfully, his proposal wasn't even that great. It definitely wouldn't go down in the history books! I think he asked me over the phone and said something along the lines of, "You wanna?" and I said, "Yeah." He could've meant "Do you wanna go to the store"!

I was so idealistic. I thought, hey, you get married and, like the fairy tales, live happily ever after. Well, certainly that's not the case and it definitely wasn't in my life. He proposed in October and I wanted a New Year's Eve wedding. I always loved that night on the calendar, because it was the end of an old year and the beginning of a new one and this would mark a new beginning for me. I told myself that I could hurry up and plan this wedding and it would be wonderful, my life would be great! People say it takes them a long time, usually a year or so, to plan a wedding. I'm here to tell you that you can do it in three weeks. That's exactly what I did, and everything was perfectly planned, down to a T.

So one of my best girlfriends and I had to coordinate flying people in and getting them hotel rooms and rental cars. And in the midst of it all, I had four—yes, four—bridal showers. I stress all this to you to point out how I was concentrating on the wrong things.

Fast forward to New Year's Eve and we have this amazingly beautiful wedding, complete with an awesome reception. Everything is great and I'm so blissfully happy that I'm finally married. We kept the ceremony under wraps because the radio station I worked at came up with the great idea that I should get married on the air. So we held off on making an official announcement on the air that I had gotten married, to plan a big event for the listening audience.

I wasn't too open to the idea at first, but what got me then, and it'll get me to this day, were the magic words "Do it for the team! It'll be great radio and good for the ratings!" I'm so in love with radio that I'll do anything for it. I know what it means to bring the audience in and have them feel like they're interacting with what you're doing.

Everybody loves a wedding. The local businesses, hotels, caterers—everything you would need to put on a great wedding—came through, and they made it special for me. So yes, we had a second ceremony, but this time it was live on the air.

The great part about it was that we got a second honeymoon out of the whole deal, in Maui, Hawaii. Who could turn that down? Mind you, my husband was not with the whole big wedding thing in general, let alone twice! Unfortunately, after both weddings were over, it was time to settle down into marriage. Things turned bad very quickly.

Michael decided to quit his job as a police officer to go work with his brother, but that failed. So with no job and no prospects, he became increasingly despondent. Not to mention that his mom passed shortly thereafter from breast cancer. It was a very sad time for him and for us, and a tough way to begin our new lives together.

Now, I wasn't perfect by any stretch of the imagination, but no matter what I tried, nothing worked. My career was flourishing. We had come off the public high from the live wedding broadcast, and despite what should've been newlywed bliss, I was going to work miserable every day.

I was losing myself in a drowning marriage. I cannot tell you enough: if a man is not working then you're going to have some problems at home. To him, that job, for the most part, defines what he is as a man.

I was the major breadwinner, so resentment set in. He couldn't handle it, and one day the intimacy and communication stopped. He didn't want me. I still wanted him, though, and it was a miserable situation.

We were only about five months into the marriage and I didn't want to be a part of it anymore. But how could I end it? It had been such a public marriage, and it all came back to bite me in the butt. I was embarrassed and ashamed. And the shame I felt caused me to stay in it.

I told myself that maybe it could work out if I tried harder, did more, was more beautiful. There had to be something I could do to make this thing work. We as women always blame ourselves, but it takes two, and the failure of that marriage was both my and his responsibility.

I was worried about what people would say, although I shouldn't have been. My family and friends had already told me not to get married. But I thought they just didn't want to see me happy. I thought they were hating on me. I had really lost my mind. So I was even more determined and told myself that I wasn't going to let the devil steal my joy!

I was quoting scripture, John 10:10: "The thief comes only to steal, kill, and destroy." I wasn't going to let that happen. I said to God, "It's on you. You've allowed me to be married, and for this to happen, so I'm in this thing now. I'm gonna stick it out!" That's what I thought I was supposed to do. But the reality is, there were plenty of scriptures I could've gone to that would've told me he and I weren't a good match. The good men in the Bible love their wives and provide for them.

I share my story with you because I don't want any woman to ever go through what I did. For any woman who has, know that I feel your pain.

Work on your relationship, nurture it, cultivate it. Be in the "moment" of the relationship. When you're in the moment, you're listening and hearing, being conscious of what's going on, and taking note and notice of what's happening. In the case of my marriage, whether we had been in the "moment" or not, we were doomed. I got married for all the wrong reasons. I'm sure, looking back, he must have felt the same way. I'll give him credit: I do think he loved me, but our marriage didn't have the proper foundation from which to grow.

Maybe if we had waited until we knew each other better. Maybe if he had gotten himself together. Maybe, maybe, maybe, maybe, maybe, whatever. It didn't work! Things got worse and worse and we moved further and further apart. Understand, before you can be in the "moment" with another person, you have to be in it with yourself. But rest assured, in my next relationship, I *will* be practicing what I preach.

You still can be a strong individual within the confines of the relationship and not lose your voice. But it certainly won't work if you allow the core of who you are to disappear. How can it? Then the person you're involved with will take it upon himself to make all the decisions. He will drive the relationship and it may be to someplace you don't want to go.

Strawberry Tip:

When you are intimate with your mate you

should never feel uncomfortable,

embarrassed, or ashamed.

CHAPTER ELEVEN

No Finance = No Romance

SUBJECT: Is Money Everything?

I met this wonderful man two months ago. He is caring, considerate, and a great father. In the beginning we went out on dates, to the movies, out for drinks, and we had amazing conversations and chemistry, which led to more dates. Then he would act too tired to go out or he'd say, "Maybe we should stay in and watch a movie." Well, after three weeks of this I became bored out of my mind! We have talked every day since meeting and he admitted that he is broke and that he took out a loan for us to date the first month. To me money is not everything, but then he asked to borrow money from me.

Don't worry, Shirley, it's not going to happen! He constantly complains about not having money, which is a total downer. My suggestion was that he find another job, one where he works five days a week instead of three or four, but then he complains he would not be *able to spend time with his son, which is admirable but confusing. How does one get used to being broke? So much so you don't even try for better? Should I continue this relationship and hope he finds a better job or move on to someone more equally yoked?*

I've been raised to believe that the man should be the provider in a relationship. It's the 21st century and times are definitely different. There are a lot of women making more money than men. Unfortunately, many couples are just out of sync on this whole money issue.

Finances are the number one reason, according to many statistics, that couples break up. (Next is sex.) A lot of people are pulling credit reports on each other at the beginning of their relationships because they want to know the history of the person they're dating.

Check out this letter from a husband who wrote to the show for help.

Subject: My Wife Is Sending Us to the Cleaners

I am a 48-year-old man who has been married for seventeen years. My wife and I love each other dearly, but we just don't see eye to eye on anything anymore. We have four kids and are struggling to make ends meet. Our debt-to-income ratio is in the red. We have tried to make it work.

My wife is so stubborn. She won't listen to me and continues to dig us deeper into debt. I love her to death, but I'm tired of giving and giving but not receiving. She gets mad when I get on her case, and we know how it is when a woman is mad! I try to avoid doing that just to keep peace. If I divorce her I'll be broke and probably forced to live with my mom. I'd rather die than do that, but if I stay then I'm unhappy for eternity. What can I do?

Bottom line, you have to know who you're marrying. It's not only about them paying the bills either, it's about them paying the bills *on time*. It doesn't matter to me who pays the bills as long as they get paid. And whoever can manage the money the best in the relationship should have that responsibility.

But if a man is broke, you have two choices, either cut your losses or try to help him get on his feet. You can do the latter by encouraging him and suggesting how he can enhance his skills and talents, and even helping him with his job search. However, I don't suggest encouraging him to go into deeper debt, or footing the bill while he chills.

On the other hand, I think it takes a really strong man to deal with a woman who makes more than him. But that woman can't be throwing it up in his face all the time.

Anything can be negotiated—it's all in the way you handle it. You have to make sure you have common goals when you enter into a relationship.

As I mentioned, the fact that I made more than my husband figured into my marriage ending, and in the journey of trying to process it all I said that the next time I was in a relationship I would let a man be a man, which to me at the time meant only dating someone who was on my level financially.

That's probably why I've stayed dateless for so long after my divorce. I thought that all men who made less money than I did were intimidated by me. That made me take a callous approach when it came to money and relationships. I said, "Hey, I don't care what that man needs, I won't give him anything." I decided if a man can't do this, or a man can't do that, then I don't need him. I'm not settling!

But that was the wrong attitude. I ended up having to adjust my thinking. I couldn't let what happened in my marriage harden my view on money as it related to men.

The reality is that men have egos and they want to be the kings of their castles, and I totally get that. Growing up, I didn't have a father in my life, but the women in my family always held their men in high esteem. I tried my best to do the same in my marriage.

For instance, when we had big family dinners for the holidays, the men were always served first. I carried that tradition into my adult life. Even though some of the women worked, when they came home they took care of their men. Bottom line, I think that's one of the keys to a successful marriage. Be feminine. Don't try to be a man. Just be a woman and all that that embodies.

Just because you have to be aggressive when you're at work doesn't mean you have to bring that same energy into the home. In a marriage you have to work together to attain and achieve certain goals.

I realize in these hard economic times you may have to be willing to adjust your philosophy of who is the provider in the home. Men and women have to give each other a break when the financial scales are unbalanced. Most important, when it comes to finances there has to be clear, upfront communication so that each person knows what to expect and what his or her responsibility and contribution is.

Strawberry Tip:

Even if you make more money than your

man, you still have to be a woman

and let the man be a man!

CHAPTER TWELVE

Stay on Your Game

SUBJECT: Stop Sneaking . . . I Know What You're Doing

I am a 31-year-old mother of two and I have been married over seven years. I have noticed that the "relations" between my husband and me have decreased to almost nothing. I have to almost coax him into having relations.

We average three times a year and my aunt was amazed as to how I even got pregnant not once but twice. Anyway, I remember Steve saying a while ago that even when men are ill they still want to have sex. Here's the problem: I think my husband is addicted to porn. I know his password and found evidence of it on his computer.

I notice that in the middle of the night he makes a trip to the hall linen closet to obtain a washcloth. I mean, I am not stupid; I know what he is doing. I once found over a hundred porn tapes and DVDs in the basement. My question to you is: What can I do to change his

interest from the computer to me? I have to mention I am a very at-
tractive young lady and have the opportunity at any time to have my
needs met outside the marriage. But he is the father of my children
and I love him and would not do that. I want to have relations with
him and only him. And I want him to stop using all my washcloths!!!

First off, if your man has an addiction to porn he has a serious problem and needs professional help. The woman in
the letter is at her wit's end. Plus, she is making it clear that she
still "has it," as evident by the outside interest she's attracting.
I'm sure underneath all that frustration she's confused, dis-
turbed, and hurt by her husband's behavior. She makes it
known that she still loves him, and still wants to be intimate
with him.

She needs to demand he go to counseling, because just like
drugs and alcohol are an addiction, sex can be, too. That's why
porn is a billion-dollar industry.

She needs to confront him about the situation. She may
even have to go to the extreme of blocking the credit card ac-
cess for that kind of service to force him to go cold turkey. It
wouldn't hurt to make an emergency visit to the pastor either!

These things are tough, but the reality is that marriage does
take work. In no way am I blaming this woman for her man's
Internet porn habit, because there are reasons men stray that
have nothing to do with the wife. They could be psychologi-
cally rooted in a bad childhood experience, or issues with
abandonment. Who knows what they are. However, you
should do whatever it takes, within reason, to keep your mate
interested. Ladies, you know what that means. We've heard it

said many, many times: Keep yourself together. Don't let yourself go just because you've got the man!

Still do the same things that you were doing before you met him. Don't get too comfortable. Don't give him a reason to cheat, whether it's with another woman or a porn website! Men also have to stay on their jobs or they'll be handing their woman over to another man.

I'm not going to sit here and tell you that it is easy to keep the flames burning in a relationship. Life has its ups and downs: you don't like your job; you've gained too much weight; you're overworked; you don't exercise like you should; the kids are getting on your nerves; or you've suffered great loss in your life.

Whatever the reason, life is hard, but don't let that be your excuse to cheat or seek out temporary thrills elsewhere. That's not a good enough reason. Yes, we're human and we have human frailties and sometimes you are tempted and stuff happens. But let's be better than that. Cheating is too easy! Let's fight for love.

When I read letters like this one I wonder if couples today have simply lost the "passion."

I had a really good girlfriend who passed away. I was actually in her wedding, and she and her fiancé argued so much, even on the day they got married. On their wedding day they were cursing each other out. But when she walked down that aisle and they started their vows, you never saw so much love.

I loved their relationship. I loved the passion and the high drama. It was fun to watch. I wondered, How can these two people who cuss and fuss like they do be so in love? But that was just their relationship. I loved being around them when they fought, and I would encourage their tiffs. I was *that* close of a friend. I would be in the middle, saying, "Are you gonna take that?" or "Did you just hear what he said?" Just for my own entertainment.

I knew it wouldn't go any further than that, because they loved each other so much. I lived vicariously through them. I wanted to be in a relationship with that type of intensity.

To me, my girlfriend and her husband had "good" arguing and "good" back and forth. That kept their relationship interesting and exciting. You saw the love. You saw the way he looked into her eyes. He might tease her and walk up and tap her on the butt. You saw the way she so carefully fixed his plate at dinner. They nurtured and took care of each other.

Now, if he didn't have the right cut of meat on his plate they might argue about it. She'd still give him his food though, and maybe after dinner they would have the greatest lovemaking sessions ever! I don't know, because I wasn't there for that, but you could tell! It was all good, though, because a relationship's got to be built on love in order for these arguments to be worked out. Theirs definitely was.

The Bible tells us not to let the sun go down on our anger. I truly believe in that. I don't want to go to bed mad and I don't think couples should either. So find the passion and even get a little drama in your lives, but don't let it fester.

Also, remember what *used* to excite you about your man or your woman. You can't be all about work or the kids. Men and women have to take the time to work together on the relationship. If you don't do it and just let things go, then your relationship may suffer dire consequences.

Strawberry Tip:

Don't get too comfortable and just hand your man over to another woman.

CHAPTER THIRTEEN

Shame on You, Shame on Me

SUBJECT: I Gave It Up, Now He Won't Leave!

I'm 39 years old and married to an older man who has a college-age son from a previous marriage. To make a long, sordid story short, my stepson's best friend has been after me for about a year. Every opportunity he could, he would flirt with me. I even told my husband that I didn't like having him around the house.

Well, my husband and I were going through some rough times and he cheated on me. My stepson's friend caught me at my most vulnerable moment and, yes, I did it. I slept with him. That was several months ago. The only thing that made me feel better about the situation is that he was supposed to graduate from the college where my husband coaches, but he has decided to stick around.

He's at our home more often than ever! He's got some kind of fatal attraction thing going on. The latest episode was at a family BBQ. He

touched me in an inappropriate area and when I looked up my
husband was looking right at us. My husband is CRAZY jealous. So
for him not to have said anything scares me. I feel as if he's cooking
something up.

The boy follows us to church and everything. I looked behind me
last Sunday and there he was, waving and smiling at me. I really
don't know what to do other than pack my bags and get out while I
can. I know he's telling people too, because my stepson, who used to
adore me, barely speaks to me now. PLEASE HELP!

Steve and I got into it over this particular letter. He was mad
at me for saying that I understood why she did what she
did and for not being bothered by the woman cheating with
someone who was so young. Is revenge a good thing? No, but
sometimes you get in that space where the pain is too much to
bear, and "acting out" is the only thing that can make it better
for you. I'm certainly not saying her actions were okay, but I
empathized with the woman. C'mon, admit it. We've all
thought about sweet revenge. I stressed that this woman repent and ask God for forgiveness. Can this marriage be saved?
I'm not sure. She betrayed not only the trust in her marriage
but her bond with her stepson as well. Once trust is broken, as
I experienced firsthand in my own marriage, it can be hard to
regain. It can be done, but you have to work twice as hard to
get it back. Some people never do and their relationships never
recover. Don't gamble with trust, you will almost always lose.

We get so many letters about cheating and infidelity. We
even get them from the "other woman." The reason I think
"The Strawberry Letter" has been so successful is because
what I say to listeners is coming from life experience. I've never

admitted it on the air, but I speak from both sides of the fence. I've been cheated on, and I've been that "other woman." I'm not proud of it and I would never encourage a woman to put herself in that position.

If a man is willing to step outside of his marriage, of course he'll say that his marriage isn't going well. He'll say whatever he needs to to get with you. But if you value yourself and have strong self-esteem, you'll see that being with a married man is a no-win position. You have no real voice, no real power in the "relationship." It's a very lonely and empty place. And like I did, you have to learn that you are worth so much more than that.

I know I've opened a can of worms, but sometimes you have to put yourself out there and come clean in order to stress a point. My affair went on for a couple of years, but finally I broke free and was able to say, "No, I can't do this anymore." It took so long because it felt good. Lust is a sin and sin feels good. Shocking, isn't it? That's a terrible thing to say, and I'm sorry, but I'm human. I hate talking about it, but I want you to know that I am writing from my experience. I lived it.

I had good friends who didn't judge me, but they were honest with me, telling me not to continue what I was doing, because he was not going to leave his wife. But a big part of how I got out was with the help of prayer. That was my wake-up call. I had to force myself to get strong enough to get out and to allow myself to hear what my friends were saying. I knew they were right. I had to stop taking his phone calls, going to meet him, and allowing him to come over. In case you're wondering . . . yes, *it* was great.

Think about your children, if you have them. Pull strength from that. If you have a daughter, like I do, then think about her. You wouldn't want her to be in a situation like that. Think about the spouse of the other party and the devastation your affair would cause her.

Have I forgiven myself? It's a horrible thing in my past, but I have. Opening up like this is embarrassing—It was a low point in my life.

If you are thinking about getting in a relationship with a married man: bottom line, cheating is wrong and 99.9999 times out of 100, no man is going to leave his wife for you. So get a grip and move on.

Sure, it's exciting at first. But after it's over you feel empty and full of regrets. I was ashamed and had to get on my knees and cry out to God.

If that man or that woman truly loves you, then wait until he or she is free and clear. That's the right thing to do. But don't hold your breath while you wait, because you'll probably turn purple and die.

Strawberry Tip:

"The forbidden fruit" is a double-edged
sword that cuts the cheater and the person
being cheated on deeply, but prayer
and good friends can help you rebuild the
self-esteem, value, and worth you've lost.

CHAPTER FOURTEEN

Security, Please

SUBJECT: Caught Up in Lies

The other day while I was in my bedroom changing my three-month-old daughter's diaper my husband's cell phone received two calls. He was sleeping so heavily that he didn't even budge. As I went to answer it, I decided to check and see what's going on in his daily phone activity.

He claims that all the numbers in his phone for women are co-workers. I went through his phone and found a text message he sent to a co-worker that he claims he doesn't even like. He told her at 7:49 in the morning how good she was looking to him. He doesn't even compliment me like that and we have been together for seventeen years!

Then I went through his picture messages and found photos of different women in his phone, naked! When I asked him about it he told me that his boy sent the pictures to him. A few days later, I confronted him with all the evidence that I had collected on him, and asked him why he put a lock on his phone. His response was that he doesn't like me looking in his phone. I told him that he acts like he's got something to hide. He replied that he's not cheating if that's what I'm accusing him of.

If he's not cheating, why lock his phone? Why have dirty pictures of women? Why lie when he always gets caught anyway? Am I wrong for looking in his phone?

I have a problem with a woman going through her man's personal belongings, looking for evidence that may or may not even be there. They're looking for trouble, and you know what they say, if you go looking . . . You know the rest. People who do this are usually insecure and bring past baggage into the relationship.

I'll admit, many years ago I found myself feeling suspicious and I started going through the things of a guy I was dating, but I stopped immediately. It just didn't feel good. I wouldn't want a man going through my personal belongings. It's a violation. And really, ladies, you have to fight off those feelings of jealousy, suspicion, and paranoia. It's not worth it. If you don't trust him, then you don't need to be with that man.

Every time you have a relationship, you're going to bring in some life experience. However, each new relationship should begin with a clean slate. Don't start a new relationship if you're still broken and jacked up from your last man. You don't want to be mad at every single man because your last one dogged you out or cheated on you.

When there is no trust in a relationship it breeds jealousy.

Men fall prey to it too. There are men who are so insecure that they get mad at their woman for being so beautiful that other men admire her when she walks in a room. If that man were secure, he would be proud of his woman and let her be the beautiful flower that she is. As long as her eyes and attention are on him, then what's the problem?

Women, we do it too! We start clownin' if another beautiful woman walks in the room and we *think* our man is scheming to holla at her. We can be dead wrong and we give that man drama and grief for nothing. We've got to start being more confident about who we are.

Another red flag is when your mate doesn't want you to talk to your family or friends. This is possessive behavior. I don't know how he can tell you who to talk to when you are both grown. So what's wrong with you? Why does this man want to isolate you? Why can't you talk to your family? He's not your daddy! He's your man! Nip that in the bud, and if you can't, then get out while you can.

Sometimes jealousy can even cause a man to hate on his woman's dreams and aspirations. Wow! Been there, done that! I can't imagine being with someone, at this point in my life, with all I've endured, who wouldn't support me. We're in this together. Why are you jealous of me if we're trying to build something for the two of us?

A jealous and insecure man has no place in my life and he shouldn't have any place in yours. You have to let him know this too. We are in these relationships for support and love and to edify and build each other up. Nothing more, nothing less.

Strawberry Tip:

**Jealousy is Cheating's evil twin; beware of
the two-headed monster.**

CHAPTER FIFTEEN

Losing It

SUBJECT: *Trying to Get Away from a Controlling Fool*

When I turned 36 I started freaking out about my biological clock. I looked at all my friends who were married and I wanted what they had. I married a guy who I wasn't necessarily "in love" with, but he said he was ready for all the things I wanted. So it was cool, because I thought I could ultimately make it work, especially after I had our son. But my husband became too possessive and controlling and I finally couldn't take it anymore.

I recently filed for divorce, but he is making it very difficult to be civil. He wants to fight for custody even though he doesn't like spending time with our son. I know he's only doing this because he wants to control me still and get back at me. I feel like I'm losing my mind. Will this madness ever be over?

I magine crying your eyes out on your way to work, back home from work, to work, from work, every day for months. I'd always heard how awful divorce was, but once I experienced it firsthand, I understood the full impact. It's one of the worst things you could ever go through. From the time that I decided to end things for good with my husband until I actually filed for divorce and began the process, I was in mourning. I felt like I was hanging on by a thread. Just like this woman, I felt like I could go insane at any given moment.

The road to divorce was a rocky one. When you're where I was, you tend to run into a lot of internal roadblocks and detours along the way. And during one of those detours, like so many times when a marriage is hanging in the balance, you'll try anything. Long story short, my ex-husband and I were separated, but thought we'd try again and got back together. That's when I got pregnant.

So there we were, trying to make it work because I was pregnant. But guess what? The love was fading. I did things like cook (yes, I cooked). I kept a clean house, I worked, I kept myself presentable, I did my hair. I tried to keep my sexy on. None of it worked.

After the baby was born we still weren't doing well. I didn't like him and didn't want to hear anything he had to say. I was just trying to keep up appearances. Two months after I learned I was pregnant, all intimacy had ceased. That's why when people ask me today how can I be celibate, I tell them that it's easy if you put your mind to it. I got plenty of practice *not* having sex when I was married!

I remember the celibacy thing came up one time when Steve and I were on air. It was around 2002 or 2003. A caller asked if

I was dating anyone, and I said no. Then she asked when was the last time I had sex. Our listeners don't have a problem getting all personal with us. So, I thought about it and I responded, New Year's Eve 1999.

That shut the room down! And I'm sure it shut down everyone in our listening audience. Steve, who, at the time, had been sitting next to me every single day for almost three years, didn't know that and his mouth dropped open. Tommy's did, too.

I further explained to everyone that I couldn't sit in this chair every day and proclaim that I'm a Christian and talk the talk without walking the walk. That was the honest to God truth, to this day. My pastor, Bishop Kenneth C. Ulmer of Faithful Central Bible Church in Los Angeles, used to say, Everybody can be celibate if you're single.

As long as you *don't* have a man or woman in your life, you can do it! Now, have I slipped up once or twice? Yes; I'm human. I'm a Christian, but I'm not a perfect Christian.

So, back to my marriage: my husband stopped initiating intimacy and when I tried to he turned a deaf ear. Well, in this case, a deaf body. I thought I wasn't attractive to him anymore. That's when I really began the whole celibacy thing. Steve and the others on the show will tease me to this day, saying, "Shirley hasn't had any since 1999!"

As I said, I've had some slip-ups, but with things like that you have to repent and ask the Lord for forgiveness and keep it movin'. I mean, if we were perfect then guess what—we wouldn't even need the Lord, so thank God He's there for us when we do make a mistake.

Finally, my husband found a job. But then he started staying out late at night and sometimes he wouldn't even come home.

So one day when my daughter, Sheridyn, was about two, I got fed up. He came home really late and it was one time too many. To top it off he fell asleep on the sofa. Why would you want to fall asleep on the sofa when you know I'm upstairs in the bedroom waiting for you to come home?

As I mentioned, we hadn't had sex since my second month of pregnancy. I'm sure any other person, man or woman, would've gone out and cheated. My husband was probably getting plenty, he just wasn't getting any at home. I suggested counseling at one point, but that's a hard one for a lot of men and he refused. So, I didn't bring it up anymore.

I had done everything I could to try and make the marriage work, but we ended up separating again. I was praying. I was fasting. I was reading scripture. I had about an hour and a half drive to work, so I let all my tears out on the way, although by the time I got there I was a complete mess.

Somehow, I'd pull it together, because even though the public can't see you over the radio, you still have to perform. I think my co-workers may have sensed something was wrong, but I'm a professional. I knew how to suck it up and put on a happy face and do my job. And then one day when I was working I had an unexpected interruption.

In addition to my co-hosting duties, I also delivered the news and traffic reports on the breaks. One of my co-workers brought me a fax, which said, "Shirley, I'm a friend of Michael's girlfriend, and she had a miscarriage last night and it was your husband's baby." Imagine someone on your job bringing you a note like that. First of all, I was embarrassed, because I knew my co-worker had read it. Secondly, I was torn apart. I had known he was out there doing something, but a baby? A baby!

I held it together. I still had to do the traffic report and the news and finish the morning broadcast. But Lord, at ten o'clock A.M., when I got off work, boy, was I a wreck. All I could think of was going to my office and calling the woman and seeing what the heck this was all about.

I talked to the woman who had sent the fax and she confirmed that she was a co-worker of the woman who had just lost my husband's baby the night before. I immediately called my husband. We were separated, but honestly, even though we had been miserable, in the back of my mind I had hoped for reconciliation. He denied everything.

He was very convincing and I wanted to believe him. I called the woman back and she gave me the number of someone else who could verify the story. As I checked further I found out it was true. I confronted my husband again and he finally admitted it. At that point it was over and there was no hope of reconciliation. I filed for divorce.

It took some time to get everything cleared up, because I didn't want to face it all. I just wanted it to go away. Poof! Just like that. I didn't want to continue to be married to him, but I didn't want to go through courts and lawyers and money. Then one of my dear girlfriends pointed out, "Shirley, you'll never be able to move on in your life unless you close this door." With those words I forged ahead, filing for divorce, and with the support of friends I got it done.

I had to meet with my husband one last time before the divorce went through to get the papers notarized. It's funny, even up to the last minute, in a friendly way, he was trying to convince me not to get the divorce. He's a nice guy, and if you met him you would love him, but it was time for it to end.

We finally got divorced, but what a bitter, angry, hurtful time for me.

Eventually I was able to admit my role in my marriage ending, which took away that bitterness because I had to take responsibility for my actions. I couldn't blame anyone else for them. If I wasn't so desperate to get a husband I could've waited until the right man came along. When you're anxious you run from man to man and never take the time to stop, look, and take heed of past mistakes.

Why be bitter when life is so short? I think you grow older faster if you're a bitter person, so why not make your life the happiest and most pleasant experience possible? If you are going through a divorce, find it in your heart to forgive your ex-spouse, because that's the only way you're going to be able to get on with your life.

Bitterness is so counterproductive and such a negative force. Why would you want that in your life? Just like we can see when people are beaming and glowing with love, bitterness can be visible in your body language, your eyes, your face. Don't think people can't see the bitterness just because you don't say anything.

You can work on it and get rid of it. We have to always look at ourselves as a work in progress. If the marriage or your life isn't what you expected it to be, work to make it better. If it can't be improved, then perhaps you married the wrong person.

I don't think every day will be sunshine and rainbows. Of course there are storms and some serious issues to get past, but you can get through them better if you're grounded and rooted in something that brings you joy. For me, God, my daughter, and my work bring me joy. What does that for you?

Strawberry Tip:

Forgive and move on.

CHAPTER SIXTEEN

Bitterness Isn't Sexy

SUBJECT: Bitter Black Woman

How do you keep from being a bitter woman? I was married for seven years. I believe that marriage is a learning experience and you grow together. We both made our mistakes, but I thought that sticking it out—even though he had a child outside of the marriage who is the same age as our daughter—and going to a thousand counseling sessions was helping us to get better. I was so caught up in keeping him, I didn't realize that not only was he cheating me out of time and love, he was cheating our four kids as well. I made excuses for me having to play both mommy and daddy roles because he was in the military. He got married a week after our divorce. He now has three stepsons and prides himself on being a good stepfather, but I don't get it, because he is not being a father to his own children. He lives in Germany, so that's his excuse for not being involved. I wanted to get to know the kids' stepmom at first but she thought I still wanted him, although I just wanted to be co-parents. Yes, I'm hurt, because of our divorce, but a man or woman comes and goes; our kids are with us for a lifetime. I just want him to love them the way I love them, they are amazing. I want to share little things they do with him and I want my kids to be a part of his family. Our kids are seven, six, four, and three. How does a man all of a sudden fall in love with someone else's kids and doesn't know his own?

I got through the physical part of dissolving my marriage much better than the emotional aftermath of it. The hurt, bitterness, and anger manifested in another way. I started saying mean and nasty things about my ex-husband when I was on the radio. I'd talk badly about him, calling him a deadbeat dad, among other things. I made sure to throw my digs in every time we got a call-in on the show that related to marriage or relationships. I was a girl behaving badly and at first, it felt good.

After a while I started saying to myself, "Hey, this failure can't be all his fault. It takes two." Then I started on my journey of self-realization. I asked myself: What was your role in the dissolution of your marriage, Shirley? Why did you marry him in the first place?

I realized that I sounded kind of stupid going off on him on-air, because if he was *so* awful, what was I doing with him in the first place? I was making myself look bad as well. And I knew that I couldn't continue to talk negatively about my child's father. No matter what went on between the two of us, this was her father, whom she loved very much.

I knew in my heart that I shouldn't ever have married

Michael. I knew we were not right for each other. Why did I forge ahead? I look back at that time and I remember feeling like God had opened every door possible for me to make the right decision. That's why it was so easy to plan a wedding, stress-free, in three weeks. God allowed it to happen. Evidently He wanted me to learn something.

I began searching, going to church. I even went to a few therapists to find out what was going on with me. What I realized was that I had just wanted to be married at the time. I thought it was the right thing to do because I wasn't getting any younger. But I got married for all the wrong reasons. Read the Bible. It gives you some guidelines to follow, and I didn't follow any of them.

1 Corinthians 13 talks about love being kind and patient. There was nothing kind or patient about our marriage.

The Bible also says that a man should love his wife as Christ loved the Church. He didn't love me like that and we didn't follow those teachings. Of course, I read them after the fact. I should've read them beforehand. We should've gone to premarital counseling, but we didn't do that either. Ladies, I think we should all take marriage a lot more seriously. Start by doing some marriage homework before you pick out your wedding dress.

I just wanted to *do* marriage. Full steam ahead with blinders, just grab a husband! That's exactly what I did, without putting any thought behind it. Big mistake.

I actually called my ex and apologized for saying bad things about him on the air, because he had heard about what I had done. How could he not? We broadcasted all over Los Angeles.

So we made our peace, and I can truthfully say I haven't spoken a negative word about him since. I learned how to forgive by going through that experience.

Practice the art of forgiveness. Forgive yourself. That's even harder sometimes than forgiving other people. I was badgering myself for being so stupid. All the signs that the marriage was a mistake were there but I was blinded by what I thought was love. Things like marrying him to get a cute last name. There's nothing worse than being blinded by ridiculous, shallow things and not really looking at the situation for what it is.

My ex-husband and I can talk now. I still love him. He remains a nice guy, just not the nice guy for me. I haven't met that nice guy for me as of yet, but I'm hopeful. You can change your thoughts and heart. Practice the art of forgiveness. Forgive him, forgive yourself.

Strawberry Tip:

You can outlive anger, recover, and move on!

PART THREE

Family Matters

God Bless the Child

"I'll stay and watch you grow . . . I'll raise
you by myself, a one woman show . . ."

—CHERYL PEPSII RILEY
"Thanks for My Child"

CHAPTER SEVENTEEN

It Takes a Woman!

SUBJECT: I Blew Up over My Daughter, Was I Wrong?

My soon-to-be ex-boyfriend and I just had a really big argument the other night because he told me that I wasn't a "good catch." He started by saying how much he enjoys the time we spend together and how much he really likes me, and that he wants to move forward with a relationship with me. Then he starts telling me how good of a catch he is because he has no children, has never been married, has a good job, etc.

Then he says, "You, on the other hand, you're not a good catch, because you have baggage." I asked him if he was referring to my three-year-old daughter and he said yes. So I got upset and told him I DO NOT, I repeat, DO NOT, have baby daddy drama, and to never refer to my daughter as baggage, and that I was a good catch. Being a mom doesn't mean I'm not a good catch. I have a great job, and my own side business. I own my condo. I pay my bills! I have a Bachelor's

Degree and am working on a Masters. And that's what makes me a
great catch! So was I wrong to blow up at him like that? He said he
wasn't saying anything bad, that it was the truth and any man
would agree. Please help me understand this one.

The nerve of this loser! This woman is absolutely a good
catch, because of all the aforementioned things. When I
think of baggage I think of issues and problems from previous
relationships that you bring into your current relationship.

Children are just part of who you are. If a man wants to be
with you, then of course he's going to have to accept your
child as well. Basically, the man in this letter is trippin', and he's
being very disrespectful and immature in his comments.

So many women have gone through this exact same scenario. Single mothers like myself are juggling careers, or trying to further our education, *and* do the job of mommy and
daddy. Or all of the above. They work hard all day, cook, clean,
help do homework, only to do it all over again the next day.

I applaud every woman out there trying to make it happen
on her own, with a child or children, especially if the father is
no longer in their lives, for whatever reason—divorce, death,
or maybe he just wasn't man enough to stay.

This letter actually takes me to a deeper place, triggering
thoughts about not just my life as a single mother, but about
my mother. When you work hard and do the best you can and
love your children, you stand up for them. That's what you
have to do. My mother did that every day for her children and
I admire her resilience, despite all the adversity she faced and
the pain she endured. As difficult as my divorce was, it doesn't
compare to what my mom went through.

My mother didn't have a choice in being a single parent. At 25 she suffered an unthinkable loss when my father was killed. She had taken me on vacation down south to Arkansas to visit my grandparents for two weeks and learned of his death upon her return.

To make matters worse, she was not only left with this little baby, but was also unable to get clear information about his death. All she knew was that a car full of white kids had struck him when he was crossing Lakeshore Drive in Chicago. How he got on Lakeshore Drive and why he was walking there, no one knows to this day.

That's not exactly a street that a black man from the South Side of Chicago would choose to take a late-night stroll on after being out on the town. I'm sure he'd probably had a few drinks. During that time it wasn't unusual for some men to work hard all week, get paid on Friday, and their families not to see them till Sunday or Monday. So it was typical for him to go out on the weekends. I can't belive my mom put up with that.

Of course, during the two weeks we were away, my mother and father spoke on the phone, but there were no cell phones back then. You talked on the phone when you could.

My parents and I were living with my father's parents in their home at the time, until our house was ready. My mom and dad were preparing to buy a two-family flat next door. We returned on Monday and my father had been missing since Saturday night. He had apparently gone out with a male co-worker, but not even the friend could give them much infor-mation. My paternal grandparents were right there in Chicago and didn't know what had happened to their own son.

Imagine all these years later and still not having closure

about this. My mother never even really talked with me about my father's death and how it impacted her until now. Did my father suffer or did he die instantly? Did anyone try to help him? How was he found? What happened to his friend? What really happened that night? There are so many unanswered questions.

When I told my mom I was writing this book, I asked her to describe the last time she saw my father alive. I imagined what he looked like, even his smell, his smile, what it was like when he held me in his arms as a baby, what his voice sounded like. I tried to feel my father's presence.

She cleared the lump in her throat and began to speak slow and steady. "It was when he drove us to the train station," she said sadly. There was a pause. I didn't press her, but I could tell she felt like talking a little more about him. I think the surprise and shock of me asking was what triggered the floodgates to open.

She began to describe her more joyful memories of seeing my father in the evenings. She told me in an upbeat tone that when she came home from work every day he was usually lying on the sofa reading the paper, since he got home from work before she did.

He worked at the Continental Box Company in Chicago. She fondly recalled to me how when she would return from a day's work, she would walk around to the side of the house to go in. There was a long walkway that ran parallel to the house. She would always peek in through the window, and there he'd be on the couch with the newspaper in hand.

Her mood turned somber at that point, as she recounted how when she had returned from the trip down south she peeked in the window and he wasn't there. At that moment, she knew something was wrong and it couldn't be good. Now, she still got up and went to work that morning, despite no one in the family knowing anything about my father's whereabouts. However, she had been worried all day, hoping for the best. As she approached the front door, her stomach was in knots. Had her hopes been in vain?

My grandfather, Papa Fred, met her at the door and told her that my father was dead. Papa Fred said that he had heard on the radio that an unidentified negro man had been killed on Lakeshore Drive. Since my father had been missing a couple of days, he checked into the report and confirmed it was my father.

Having this kind of deep and emotional conversation with my mom made me appreciate her so much more. I had never before considered the loneliness, the panic, the whirlwind of life-changing events that she must've experienced in a split second. It could've destroyed her, but she held on to her faith and stayed strong for her children.

So this process has been very cathartic. I believe hearing my mother talk about my father's passing, as limited as the information is, helped me to find closure on something that has haunted me all my life. Who was my father?

How strange is it that as I was growing up, not only was my father not there, but it was almost as if he never existed? In my mind he didn't exist, because I have no recollection of him. I was a year old and my father had literally vanished with scarce detail. There had always been a major void in my life where he was concerned.

I do think his absence may have affected my relationships

with men, or lack thereof. It's not that I have a problem attracting a man, I've just never had a good relationship with a man, whether it was moving too quickly or simply not knowing how to get what I wanted from him.

One of my biggest concerns for my daughter is that, although her father is in her life, she doesn't see him every day. She recently told me that she's talking to him more and I'm so happy. They don't live in the same city, and a good relationship is needed despite the distance. Now, although my daughter doesn't live with me either, we don't have the same issues. The difference is that my mother and I have had a co-parenting situation since Sheridyn was born. So, unlike her father, I'm very much a part of her daily life.

I don't want her to experience the abandonment issues that I did, thinking that just because her father ran away from his responsibilities, every man she gets involved with will do the same. For me, it's about her having healthy relationships and not having low self-esteem when it comes to men, like her mom did.

It's funny, I worry about my daughter's future with men, and she worries about me in the same way. She wants me to be happy. Sometimes if I mention that I've met a man she'll immediately give me the third degree because, she says, she's trying to get a stepdad!

So, if I could say one thing to fathers, it would be: you are so important to your child's life, to the development of that life. Mothers of course are there and we're the nurturers, we're important, and this is not to take anything away from us.

One thing that really does sadden me is that my mom is such a beautiful woman, but to this day she's still single. She did have various gentlemen callers when I was growing up. I remember she had one main boyfriend in particular throughout my adult life. They attempted to get married on three different occasions. Back then a blood test was mandatory. I think one time the blood test had expired, so they couldn't get married. In another instance, by the time they both got off work, got through traffic, and made it to City Hall, it was too late and everything was closed. I don't know what happened the last time, but whatever the obstacle was, my mother must've been so frustrated that she just said forget it. They remained friends, but they never tried again.

I guess I can understand. When your heart has been broken, like hers was after she lost my father, you see why a person may end up feeling like love disappointed her, so why even try? This prompts me to go back to the woman in the letter.

Why is it that women today are looked down upon or criticized if they have a child or children from a previous relationship, but men don't seem to get the same kind of bad rap? You always hear about "baby mama" this or "baby mama" that, and I know there are women out there creating unnecessary drama, but those are the exceptions. For the most part single mothers are like my mom was, and like I am, working hard to raise good kids.

When you have children and you meet someone it becomes a package deal! Instead of a woman being criticized for her past choices, a man should be cheering her on, admiring her strength and courage. Most women like the woman in the letter, like me, like my mother, like so many of you reading this book have to be mommy and daddy. But keep hope alive, because good men do still exist!

Strawberry Tip:

Any man who says he loves you, but doesn't

want to step up his game and support all

that you do as a single mom,

isn't the man for you!

CHAPTER EIGHTEEN

The Ties That Bind

My daughter, Sheridyn, currently lives with my mother, who has helped me raise her since birth. At the time I gave birth to my beautiful baby girl, my marriage was failing and I had a demanding career. I wasn't sure how I was going to deal with everything. But then in steps my mom, who said to me, "Look, you gotta go to work. I'll take the baby." I agreed, and next thing I knew, at three months old Sheridyn was on a plane to Arkansas with my mom.

I saw Sheridyn on a pretty regular basis, usually every two or three months. Before she started going to school, until she was about five years old, she and my mom would sometimes stay in Los Angeles with me for several months at a time. After that I would go to Arkansas for special occasions and holidays, such as her birthday, Thanksgiving, Christmas, Mother's Day, and others. After vacations with her and my mom, when I'd have to head back to work, I was crying and carrying on by the time I got to the airport.

And while allowing my mother to raise my daughter was certainly a blessing, at times I've been plagued by guilt and wondered if I made the right decision. Part of me feels that I should be the one raising her every day, while the other side is happy that I have the freedom to be able to focus on my career one hundred percent, worry-free, so I can provide for my daughter.

Recently I asked Sheridyn to consider moving in with me full-time. I knew she was comfortable living with my mother and didn't want to disrupt her life or put any pressure on her. She wrote her own Strawberry Letter on the topic to tell me how she feels:

Subject: Torn Between the Big City and the Country

Dear Mommy,

I want to start by saying you are the GREATEST! It has been extremely hard to choose between you and Granny. I love you both dearly, which I hope you both know. My grandmother is elderly and needs assistance, plus I've been with her basically my whole life. But even though we have had great years together, I now have the desire to be with you. This is where the hard part comes in.

You live in a fast city, with nice cars, beautiful people, and everything you could imagine! Arkansas is country with country people, but you know what? I LOVE IT.

It's my home, and my entire family is basically here, but where you live seems like where I belong. I love being with you. We have the best times together. We shop, go to movies, get our nails and hair done. I'm exposed to more things I love there, especially the music and cars and of course clothes!

I love Arkansas, and I love where you live. What should I do?? I don't want to hurt anyone.

> *Sincerely,*
> *Sheridyn*

It took me a few days to process her words. I couldn't believe Sheridyn actually wrote them. My baby is growing up so fast. But an answer finally hit me in the middle of the night:

Dear Sheridyn,

Baby, what a tough position we've put you in at such a young age. This has been hard on everyone. I've tried to make the best out of the situation that I possibly could. You can't even imagine how much I love you and how grateful I am that my mother, your grandmother, has been able to help me with you all these years.

Believe me, I never planned for it to be this way. I never thought that your dad and I would get a divorce. So I always thought that you would have both parents to be with you and raise you.

You're torn, I'm torn, and your grandmother's torn. But the sad part is that you're feeling this way at such a young age. Let me commend my mother for the awesome job that she's done with you. You're a beautiful, intelligent, articulate, well-raised young lady. I couldn't be more proud of you and the way you've turned out.

Even though I haven't been there physically every day like so many mothers are, you've never missed out on the love I have for you. We may not have had the quantity of time together, but we've certainly had quality time.

I know this is not an ideal situation. If I could change it, trust me

I would, and you would've lived with me. But by me being a single parent and not being able to afford a live-in nanny, it was just kind of hard. So that's where your grandmother stepped in and helped me. As a result, you and your grandmother have developed such an incredible bond.

I just want you to know how much I love you and that everything I do is for you. I sacrifice being with you to do for you. Maybe that is not the greatest decision, but that was the best choice I could've made under the circumstances. I hope you'll be able to forgive me for not being with you every day, but I definitely want you to know that it's not because I don't love you, and that I did try to be the best mother I could possibly be.

I was okay with her decision to stay with my mother, and she's going to live with me once she starts high school. My priority is her happiness. Did it make me feel sad that she chose to stay with my mother rather than live with me? A little.

It tore me apart to be away from my child. There are some things that still bother me about making the decision thirteen years ago to let her go live with my mother. For example, I missed Sheridyn's first steps. My mom had to tell me about it over the phone. I saw her crawling, though, and I'll never forget when she first smiled at me. I also missed her first words—but it's okay, because she talks a lot now, and she's definitely made up for it! Sometimes Sheridyn would call her grandmother "Mom," but my mother would always correct her.

I missed some important developments in her life, but those are the sacrifices that I have to accept. God willing, I will be there for the next round of firsts—first date, first serious relationship, first heartbreak. These things are important too as she grows into young womanhood.

Just because your parent or parents are helping you raise your child does not mean you're a bad parent. It doesn't matter who is helping you raise your children, just be active and have a presence in their lives. If your child is in the same city as you, then that's great, but if they're in another city, then you have to work that much harder—phone calls, letters, e-mails, frequent visits, whatever you need to do to make it happen.

Things don't always go as planned in life. However, I've realized through my co-parenting journey with my mom that families come in different forms. We have to see the blessing even when we're forced to alter the plan!

Strawberry Tip:

Love and communication are the keys to

making any family work.

CHAPTER NINETEEN

Make the Grade

SUBJECT: Am I Being Too Hard on My Son?

I'm a single mother raising a son, and sometimes I feel as if I'm never doing enough to be a good parent. I'm angry because my baby's daddy isn't around and I have to be both mother and father. It's tough out here. I want my son to be able to succeed in the world and I can't depend on his daddy for that support. I've been pushing him a lot lately to do well in school, and I'm worried I'm putting too much pressure on him.

My daughter, Sheridyn, brought home a B one grading period. Okay, maybe a B is good, but I knew she was capable of better. As a single parent, I have to work double-time to push my child to be the best. I always tell my daughter that hard work pays off! I'm living proof.

When I was growing up, my mom had a present for me just about every day when she came home from work. She'd usually bring a sweater, socks, or a new dress or two or three.

I decided that since I wasn't in Sheridyn's life on a day-to-day basis I would carry on that tradition. Unfortunately, the gift buying got out of hand. Whatever she wanted—shoes, clothes, gadgets, the new PlayStation, iPod, whatever—I bought.

One day I happened to be shopping in Los Angeles with my best friend's mother and Sheridyn. My daughter wanted everything she saw, and I kept buying. That's how I had been operating, buying her everything and anything to "make her happy." My friend's mother stopped me dead in my tracks and said, "Stop, right now! What you're doing is wrong. You're buying out of guilt. You can't let children manipulate you like that. You're the mother and you have to say no."

It's not that I didn't ever say no to Sheridyn or discipline her, but when she looked at me with those big, pretty, puppy dog eyes of hers, I melted and bought whatever she wanted. That day in the store was a wake-up call.

I learned a valuable lesson with the help of my best friend's mother: don't get in the habit of buying things out of guilt.

Yes, my daughter was raised by her grandmother, but with strong influences and support from me, her mom. No, I wasn't there every day, but she's okay and not a moment goes by that I don't shout thanks and praise to God and my mom—and for the moment, myself.

As a single mom, I've learned that when life gives you lemons you just have to make lemonade. I never wanted to be in this position, but guess what, here I am! I have my mom as a great example, as well as other single mothers who have done amazing, outstanding jobs with their children.

It's not like it can't be done. I saw how hard my mother struggled, but she survived. My mom raised two great kids, and if I can be half the mother she was, then I'll be just fine.

So I'm going to give myself a break sometimes. To single parents everywhere, like the woman in the letter at the beginning of the chapter, give yourselves a break. Parenting is a hard job, but look at your children. If they're good kids, you're doing okay. And even if they're not good kids, because they have stumbled along the way, if you've planted good seeds in them, like the Bible says in Proverbs 22:6, "Train a child in the way he should go, and when he is old he will not turn from it," lean on that scripture and believe in it. Kids need love and time. Teach your children well and eventually they'll stick by those lessons.

Of course, sometimes outside influences can be stronger than the ones you have at home. Just do your best. And if you start to feel like you can't do it alone, then enlist the help of others. If you have a son, get a male role model, such as an uncle or male friend that you trust, to stand in the gap. Take him to church.

Remember, you're the parent. Take charge and take control!

I've even created my own mini "survival" guide for single parenting. These are things that, as the mother of a teenage girl, I wanted to share with those of you who, like me, are still learning and growing as parents:

1. Take care of your kids, but take time for yourself—take a bubble bath, for example, or give yourself a few extra minutes in the bathroom alone.

2. Be a role model—Set an example for your kids, because they mimic everything we do. If you're actin' a fool somewhere, they'll do the same. Don't take that chance!

3. Talk to them—even when my daughter doesn't like what I'm saying, I tell her, "You may not understand it, you may not even get it until you grow up, get married, and have kids of your own, but you will thank me later."

4. Listen—when I was growing up, my mother didn't allow me to have much of a voice or opinion. Her favorite line was "Because I said so." Try to keep the lines of communication open with your child, even about the little things. Then maybe they'll come to you when the *big* things occur, like boys or their bodies changing. I'm not my daughter's friend, but I am friendly with her.

5. Stay vigilant—I'm all for reading their diaries, messages on their phones, picking up the other phone in the house to hear what they're talking about. I don't knock on doors before going into Sheridyn's room. Hey, it's my house. However, she'd better knock before coming into my room. She lives here, but it's *my* house!

6. Teach your kids manners—they will get much further in life with manners. What's wrong with saying "please" and "thank you"?

7. Stress that they must always do their best—try to give your children a glimpse of the kind of life they can have if they do the right thing now and study hard in school.

8. Let a kid be a kid—I tell my daughter in a heartbeat, "If you want somebody to 'kick it' with, then go get one of

your 13-year-old friends. I'm your mother, remember that!" Don't expect them to know about life like you do. And don't bring them into grown-folks' business, plain and simple! You know what I'm saying, single parents. Don't involve your kids, or put them in the middle of drama or arguments you and your ex are having. Let a kid be a kid.

In essence, I've come a long way as a parent. It's all about trial and error, and thank God my mom is by my side! I'm sure that if given the chance to change something from our past, all of us would do so. I've often contemplated that thought as it relates to my mother raising my daughter. But the reality is that life isn't always the storybook tale we hope for.

Strawberry Tip:

There's no perfect parent and no perfect kid, and we can always find something to feel guilty about. Don't be so hard on yourself!

CHAPTER TWENTY

Stop the Madness

SUBJECT: *Jerry Springer Mess*

I recently graduated from college. My youngest brother, who was only 19 and married, died this year and I decided to move in with my mother to help pay bills and be there for emotional support. As soon as I moved in I knew it was a mistake. My mother quit her job and now stays home and smokes weed and drinks all the time. To make things worse, late at night someone always comes by the house to pick her up. I did a little investigating and found out that she has been sleeping around with my deceased brother's wife!

When I found this out I told my oldest brother and he admitted to sleeping with our brother's wife too. He also told me that he knew our mom was sleeping with her. Now, I am devastated and want to leave the house, but since I pay all the bills I have no money to get my own place. What should I do?

W hat kind of family is this? Who *does* this? This is beyond any kind of logic and reason. *I'm* embarrassed for the mother in this scenario because she doesn't sound like *she* has sense enough to be embarrassed. If I were the young man who moved in to help his mother, I would stop paying all those bills and move back out.

The letter may be extreme, but this kind of mess happens in families. I question what has happened to the family structure. Are we that lost? The next letter was equally disconcerting, and I wanted to include it because I could feel this woman's pain.

Subject: Comfort, Support, and Family

I need help with supporting my lil sister. She is 22 years old with a four-year-old son and is six months pregnant with her second child. She's the talk of the projects—from the dirty clothes she wears to the fights she and her "baby daddy" have in front of the whole projects. I don't live close by so it's not every day that she and I talk. But when we do I try to encourage her to have a new look on life.

I have tried to be real with her to get her to see that she can do better than what she's doing. I don't want to judge her or to have her feel that I'm trying to "mother" her. I just want her to realize that I've been there and done that, and I have made my share of mistakes and I don't want her to go down that same road. She has no one back home to support her. Our mom just talks about her and puts her down. She's done me the same way.

Our aunts are in no position to offer advice, because of their living conditions, and they help her peers spread the rumors and talk about her. I'm the only one in the family who actually cares about my sister's image, her well-being, and her future. How do I get her to see this? How do I get her to see her condition, and how she needs to change if she wants better? I pray for her and the rest of my family as well. How do I get the understanding across to her?

Signed, A Sister's Love

That is a powerful love right there. I have to commend this woman for caring about her sister when no one else seems to. It's as if her sister doesn't even care about herself. Sometimes, try and try and try as we may, we can't make other people see life's possibilities if they don't have the vision.

To this woman, and those who might be facing similar situations in their families, keep doing what you're doing. It's all about praying for your loved ones, talking to them—telling them that you love them and stressing they love themselves more. Not only do you need to encourage family members in this type of situation to hang with a different crowd, but maybe take them with you when you hang out with your friends.

Expose them to various experiences so they can see that they don't have to be in the types of scenarios they're in. Then a person can take the steps to move out of that situation, and go about making a better life for herself. Sometimes it's about showing them a different way. People don't hear as well as they can see, a lot of times.

When it comes to dealing with family, we women are such natural caretakers. We want to be there for everyone. That's generally our makeup and our disposition. So it's important for us to learn that at some point, no matter how much we love our mothers, fathers, brothers, sisters, whoever, sometimes there is only so much we can do.

We have to learn to say no. We have to stand up to our crazy uncle and our crazy auntie and tell them, "Hey, this is wrong, and you need to cease and desist! Stop it!" And I say to you, do these things with respect, because nine out of ten of these people are your elders. But you have to stop the madness and not let it go on to another generation.

You cannot continue to bring kids up and allow them to witness the foolishness in your family. Let the relatives who are acting a fool know they can't carry on in your house. And if you're at their house, when they start the foolishness get up and leave. Warn them that you told them you weren't going to tolerate it in your presence. Leave! Maybe they will get the message.

You know, everyone has dysfunction in their family. However, there comes a point in time that you have to shut it down if it's affecting you in a negative way. Shut. It. Down.

Strawberry Tip:

Step up, be responsible parents, and start

using the good sense God gave you

to raise your kids.

PART FOUR

Self

No More Drama

"Only God knows where the story ends for
me, but I know where the story begins . . ."

—MARY J. BLIGE
"No More Drama"

CHAPTER TWENTY-ONE

Pass the Torch

When I was little, I loved being the center of attention and running my mouth—pretty much the same thing I do today on the radio! There would be a bunch of people over to our home, and I'd be in the middle of all the excitement, running around, doing whatever. Suddenly, my mother would shout out to me from the kitchen or wherever she was, "Get somewhere and sit down, little girl, everyone has seen you." Her words made me feel like running away and hiding. They made me pull back.

I've even talked about it on the air. Of course, Steve, Carla, and Tommy tease me about it. So the running joke is that if someone is getting a little too out of hand, one of them will say, "Get somewhere and sit down, everyone has seen you." I can't say that I'm overly sensitive about it now, but it did embed in me this fear of being embarrassed or humiliated. But then again, I guess I shouldn't have gotten a job on *The Steve Harvey Morning Show,* because that happens on the regular!

Now that I'm grown up and a mother, I understand that my mom didn't want it ever to be said that her kid was in there clownin' or getting out of control. She was a very proud woman. She figured if she thought it, somebody else thought it too, so before anybody else said anything, my mom was going to shut it down.

For a long time I was quiet and kept my opinions to myself. But now, of course, it's much different, as you hear when you listen to me on the radio. But growing up I wasn't really allowed to express myself.

I encourage my daughter, Sheridyn, to express herself and I listen to her opinion on anything, be it politics or boys. She could always tell me which boy she thought was cute. Before the whole Chris Brown fiasco, she loved him, but right now she's into Justin Beiber, and I realize that these types of crushes are perfectly natural for someone her age.

When I was Sheridyn's age, if I talked about a boy, my mom would adamantly tell me that we don't talk about those kinds of things.

One thought that's always lingered in the back of my mind is whether or not the tragic loss of my father stole a piece of my mother's self-esteem. As a young woman, she was the life of the party, but after my father died, some of that liveliness she had in her spirit disappeared.

Being a young mother and widow shaped my mother's life quick, fast, and in a hurry. I remember her always being so busy;

I'd start bugging her like kids do, and she'd tell me about how she didn't have time for this or that. I began to feel abandoned by both my parents—by my father's death and my mother's emotional distance. I couldn't understand at the time.

I didn't grow up in an environment where parents and children were friendly. Parents were parents. I'm glad I can finally call my mom a friend. She's actually my best friend. But we had a rocky relationship for a few years when I was a teenager. I didn't go out and get pregnant or do drugs, but I had a smart mouth and was very disrespectful. I did whatever the heck I wanted to do. I would come in the house at whatever time I wanted to and leave when I wanted. I didn't show her respect. I was rebellious, and the relationship was combative.

We didn't have the kind of relationship that I wanted. I wanted to be able to talk to my mom and go to her with my problems, but that wasn't possible. She was very much a "because I said so" and "do as I say, not as I do" parent. I'm not saying that's a bad thing. I'm just describing what it was like for me.

As a result, we didn't communicate with each other very well. One day I said, "Mom, I can't talk to you." She turned around and said to me, "Well, I can't talk to you!" That shocked me, because I'm thinking I got it together. But guess what? I wasn't talking to her in the right way, and she probably didn't feel like fighting with her daughter on that day.

My daughter only sees how my mom and I relate to each other now and has no idea how our relationship used to be. I'm glad she and my mom communicate very well with each other. She tells my mom everything, and my mom has definitely softened up. Sheridyn and my mom are so close that they even get together and gang up on me!

I still can't believe there was actually a point when I was a young adult, when I didn't like my mother and she didn't like me. I never wanted to be a person who didn't like my mother. Let me be clear, I love and adore my mother. But I had to sit back and ask myself: Why can't I talk to her? Why can't we get along? What is really going on with me?

Then I just started putting together in my head all the stories she used to tell me about what went down when she was a child, and once I realized what she must have gone through and how difficult her life was, and how hard it was to raise two children by herself after my father's death, my heart softened. I changed my attitude toward her.

My mom was working so she could keep the house, keep the car, so that she could bring me home gifts every day. That was her way of showing me love. We had the best Christmases that you could imagine. Our Christmases could go up against the richest person's in the world. Did we appreciate it at the time? Probably not like we should have.

My mother was just doing what she knew to do. I told myself, "Hey, my mother does love me, and I need to do my part to help her be the kind of mom I want her to be." You can't change another person, but you can change yourself. That's what I did.

So, yes, when you sit down and you look at your life and your actions, you'll start forgiving a whole bunch of people. You'll see that it's not always the other person's fault that the relationship isn't working out. Sometimes you need to get yourself together.

Strawberry Tip:

Release your past in order to raise your
children to be confident today and to know
their power in the future.

CHAPTER TWENTY-TWO

Do You Like What You See?

I spend so much time in my bathroom, I often say to my friends that I think the secret to a good marriage would be separate bathrooms. That's where I have my "me" time.

That's where I get to look in the mirror and not just pluck my eyebrows, but really look at who I am, or who I've become, or who I'm becoming. There were times in my life when I didn't like to look in the mirror. I wouldn't even glance when I walked past. When I think back, I guess I must've been going through some pretty hard times. Maybe I was in one of those bad relationships and I couldn't face myself.

Sometimes you've got to make yourself look in the mirror, and if you don't like what you see then you've gotta do something about it. That's the beauty of things. As long as you have breath in your body, you can change yourself and evolve—and, of course, you can thank God for that.

When you look in that mirror, do you like the person looking back? Do you even recognize her? Is she happy? When you look at your eyes, do they look sad or tired? Do they look worried? Really study your reflection.

If you don't recognize yourself, as I so often have not when I've done that exercise, then it's time for you to start working on something—yourself! If you don't like the way you look physically, well then, you know you need to get in the gym. If your skin isn't looking right, then you know you need to lay off the soda, start drinking more water, and maybe even change your skin care regimen.

Now, that deals with the outside, but what about the inside? If you see that your eyes look sad, you've got to figure out what's happening. How did you get to this point?

Lately, I've been running from that dark cloud of depression. Being single and alone is tough for me. There are times when I want to be with someone, have a mate or a husband, and it's hard when you look around and everyone's all "boo'ed up." Sometimes I think I want a dog, but I'm terrified of animals, so that won't do!

Basically, here's the chain of events: If I think about the fact that I'm alone and I'm at home by myself, I'll eat. If I eat and don't exercise, I'll gain weight, and then I won't want to go out. If I don't go out, then I won't meet anyone. If I gain more weight, I'm not gonna ever want to go out because I'm too fat. If I'm too fat, I get depressed.

That's the vicious cycle I live. I know it needs to be broken, and I'm working hard on myself to capture that light that will pull me through, and hold on to it.

When you look in the mirror and don't recognize yourself,

you are at a dangerous point. The last time I was really pleased with the Shirley looking back at me in the mirror, I had gone on a total body cleanse. I drank fresh juices and water all day. My skin and my hair were beautiful. I had lost weight. And I had mental clarity. My relationship with God was really at a high point. Right now I'm not quite at that state, but I am holding on to that image and I'm slowly working back toward it. I liked how I felt about myself.

At some point in this journey we call life, we have to get to know ourselves better—our likes, our dislikes, who we are, what we can tolerate, what we can't, what others can or won't put up with, etc. You've got to do some deep thinking and go into prayer. You've got to talk to God and read His word. You've got to talk to and be around people you like, and who share common interests with you. The goal is to keep the MBS (mind, body, and spirit) in sync. Always strive to do that!

Strawberry Tip:

Work toward loving how you look, from the inside out.

CHAPTER TWENTY-THREE

Where Is Your Faith?

Over the years, many people asked me about writing a book. I've contemplated doing so many times. I kept saying, "Why me? Who's gonna read my book? Who wants to hear what I have to say?" I'd even get myself all pumped up to start the writing process, and suddenly I'd second-guess myself and say forget it.

I mean, I work next to Steve Harvey. People listen to him with such anticipation. I do too, and I sit next to him! But then I thought, What if just one person picks up *my* book and it changes them? Maybe I can inspire someone with my message.

Even as I'm finishing this book, my heart is racing. It's a scary thing, but I've done it! Come what may!

I'm a work in progress, even at this age. I don't have it all together. Oh, you thought I did?

I gave a big, fat, elaborate prayer the morning I started

working on the book, as I had the night before. I thanked God for this opportunity and asked Him to work through me, give me the words, give me favor, and bless not only my mind, but my co-author's as well. It occurred to me that writing a book is like giving birth.

I remember when I was in the delivery room about to have my daughter and they were getting ready to stick the IV in me. I was actually more afraid of the IV than having the baby. I was terrified—no, petrified! How crazy is that? My mother was in the room with me. She saw how I was freaking out and she said four very important words to me that got me through it: "Where is your faith?"

Right then I stopped panicking. A calm came over me. I did exactly as those doctors told me, and the fear melted away.

That was it. Those four words got me through labor. I don't even think my mother knows the impact she had on me by telling me that. It was October 19, 1996, and from that point on I understood what faith was. You can't profess to be all you say you are and not walk in it and not exercise it. That's why I now carry those words with me in my heart.

I have a picture in my bedroom of a boat shipwrecked in a terrible storm. I bought it because it reminds me that, yeah, there are storms in life, but we get through them.

It's important we know that even if our fathers have left the earth, or if they haven't been a part of our lives for whatever reason, we still have a Heavenly Father to depend on. The good thing about having a relationship with God is that He doesn't mind if I have a man in my life! But also know that your Heavenly Father doesn't keep your bed warm at night, or help you bring the groceries inside the house from the car, or help you with the bills. You need an earthly man to do those things!

To every woman reading this book, it's imperative that you have a relationship with God. I'm not saying that you have to go to church every Sunday, but you do need to develop your relationship with Him. He's always available to you.

You don't like it when someone comes to your home unannounced, do you? Well, God is not going to come over unannounced. He lets you know that He's there but He wants you to open the door and ask Him in. That's how much He respects you. He wants to be invited in, just like you would invite a guest to your home.

And ladies, it's okay if you've been "out there." You think God doesn't know that? So many of us would probably like to reach out or call on Him but we feel our lives have been so horrible and so shameful and we've done so many despicable things that we don't know how to call on God. But it's as simple as, "Hey, God, I need you."

Strawberry Tip:

Always keep God first and take Him with

you wherever you go!

Shirley's Strawberry Letter To Self

SUBJECT: Help, I Can't Believe I'm Still Single!!!

Dear Shirley,

    I'm a divorced, attractive, mature woman who seems to have it all together. I own my own home and car. I have a beautiful daughter and a wonderful career. However, I am single and have been for quite a few years. I never thought in a million years that I would end up alone with no one to call my own. I must admit that some of it is my fault because I neglected to make having a man a priority in my life. It's almost as if I've given up on ever finding true love and am content to be by myself. How did I get here??? Please advise as to how I can break out of this wall I seem to have built around myself and my

*heart. I want to meet the man of my dreams or at least start dating
again!*

Signed,
What's a girl to do?

P.S. I refuse to settle!

These letters always start off so nicely, don't they? Let me
commend you on your accomplishments first: you have a
beautiful daughter, a wonderful career, and some nice material
things.

Congratulations. But those things can't keep you warm at
night. They can't ask you out on a lunch or dinner date or take
you on a romantic vacation, and they can't bring you flowers
or rock your world!

Well, Shirley, as long as you have breath in your body it's
never too late to find love. I don't think you should settle either!! But it's going to take effort on your part. If you are serious about getting a man, start going to the gym if you don't go
already, because nothing builds confidence like looking and
feeling good about yourself. Men love a confident woman.

And you must start going out. That's where the men are.
You have to mingle and flirt a little bit. You can try online dating too if you're brave enough. Ask your friends to hook you up
with their single friends and accept all invitations. You never
know where you might find Mr. Right. You have no more time
to waste. He's out there but doesn't know where you live. Get
out of the house, where he can find you, and you can give him
your address and the key (to your heart).

You deserve a good, loving relationship. You may have kissed a lot of frogs, but leave that bitterness and baggage in the past—it isn't sexy. If you have taken the proper inventory of who you are, what you want out of a relationship, and what you can offer, have great friendships and are confident in who you are, and have a sound spiritual foundation, then you are a great catch for any man. Know your value and open your heart to new possibilities.

Sincerely,
Ms. Shirley Strawberry

More of "The Strawberry Letter"!

I couldn't resist sharing the following letters, which I certainly found hard to forget, and which have become fan favorites. I hope you find these as entertaining—and illuminating—as everyone on *The Steve Harvey Morning Show* did.

SUBJECT: Dirty Old Man

Dear Steve and Shirley:

If someone would've told me my 75-year-old ex-friend was a sex pervert, I would have thought that person was telling a lie. But the truth has come out! One night I was on my computer looking for recipes, and my friend's name popped up on my screen saying he was available. I sent him a note saying "hi," and surprisingly he responded provocatively. I realized he did not know it was me, because he began to ask my bra size and sexual positions that pleased me, and telling me he was excellent in bed. He described his way of performing sex as one that would make a woman scream and beg for more. This dirty old man never asked my name. I was shocked. I could've been any random woman on the Internet. He went on to talk about how he wanted to put his mouth in places that I won't repeat! Very disgusting. I've since ended the relationship and never want to see him again. How can a 75-year-old man be so disgusting? What makes it so sad is this man goes to church every Sunday and proclaims to be a Christian. Did I do the right thing by cutting him off?

My first reaction to this letter was that this woman had to be pretty "mature" herself to be dating a 75-year-old man. And there's nothing wrong with that. So, I can understand how upset she is that now that she's seeing a side of him that she didn't know: his sexual perversion. She absolutely is doing the right thing by letting him go. He's probably a harmless old man, but you can never be too sure the way people conduct themselves over the Internet nowadays. The sad statistics in our communities reflect that AIDS among black women are staggering, but particularly older black women. So, I say yes, this woman did the right thing by leaving this dirty old man alone. She needs to go out and find her a nice, respectable, and safe mature man and keep it movin'!

Subject: Finally Found My One True Love

Dear Shirley and Steve,

A few months ago I met the most amazing man during my lunch break. Since then we have had lunch together every day, which has graduated to dinner. He has even cooked for me, and I've met his family and friends. They love me, and I love them! For the past six months he's been speaking of taking this relationship to the next level, which to him means living together and perhaps marriage. I've never felt like this before—ever. I'm head over heels in love with this man. But the problem with all of this is that I am married with two children. I'm not in love with my husband. We got married because I was pregnant, and for the past seventeen years I kept my head down, stayed on my grind, raised two kids, ran a household, and managed a career. I accepted my life and my marriage for what it was and never expected anything more. I never thought that I would ever get lucky enough to feel love on this level. Now I'm in my forties and in love for the very first time in my life. I love my family, but do I leave my husband or do I leave my love? I am in somewhat of a quagmire and in dire need of advice. Please help!

Right now, this woman has to do the right thing and leave her "love" alone because she's still married. I hate that she even started up a relationship with this man. In order to make this so-called dream come true she has to divorce her husband. I don't usually tell people to divorce, but obviously she's unhappy. In short, she needs to handle her business at home. Karma is not something you want to play with!

Subject: My Baby Won't Make Love to Me Anymore!

Dear Steve and Shirley,

I am a man who has been in a relationship with a woman for about a year and a half. I'm 32, and she is 27. Everything was going great until she recently dropped a bomb on me. She does not want to have sex with me anymore. When we first started dating she told me she was a "virgin." However, it only took us about two months to have sex. Everything was going great. Until now, I felt that this was the woman I was going to marry. We talked of marriage, and being realistic I told her that it would take maybe another two years to get our finances right before we made it official. She seemed to be okay with that goal. Then one month ago she comes up with this idea that she wants to be celibate until she gets married. My jaw dropped. I was hit hard, trying to figure out what I had done. Could it be that she thinks I'm not the one anymore? She tells me she's been going to church and they told her to stop having sex. Now, mind you, she is 27 but goes to teen Bible study. It seems a little odd to me that a grown woman would be in a class with people half her age. She says the adult Bible study doesn't talk about anything that interests her. Sex seems to be the only thing she wants to change. She sees nothing wrong with drinking, going to the club with her girlfriends, or wearing revealing outfits a la Beyoncé or Rihanna. How can you wear tight Beyoncé jeans in front of me, sleep in the same bed with me, and not expect me to be busting at the seams or upset about it? I know that she says her decision is God-based, so I feel as if I have no argument. But I didn't even get a warning. Just one day and boom. No more sex. I'm waking up in the middle of the night like I'm 14 years old with sex dreams, and she's sleeping like a baby. I know sex isn't everything but I feel like I'm losing my connection to her. I don't want to leave her. What do I do?

First off, it's true the Bible says not to have sex before marriage. So, she's right in telling him that her church is teaching the practice of celibacy. I guess she's only trying to follow what's really the Christian way, as far as sex goes. However, in terms of her sleeping in bed with the man and getting him all excited—that's wrong and unfair. Maybe what she's really trying to do is cut him off so he'll think twice about that idea he had to wait two years to marry her. She might think going cold turkey in the bedroom will speed up the marriage proposal process. He may want to reconsider his original plans or prepare for a long winter!

Subject: I Slept with His Nephew, Now I'm Pregnant!

Good morning, Steve and Shirley,

I am a 38-year-old woman, and church mess has caused a world of trouble for my family. My husband is a church pastor and there is this one particular elderly lady in her eighties who started a rumor that two years ago my husband had fathered a child by her daughter. I confronted my husband about the whole situation, and he denied it. Of course I didn't believe him, because why would this elderly woman need to tell lies about him? I was so hurt and upset about the whole situation that I decided I would get back at my husband by sleeping with his 23-year-old nephew. Wow, that was a mistake. Now I cannot get him to leave me alone. He constantly calls and texts me. I have told the nephew that it was just sex, but he can't seem to get the picture. To make matters worse, I have found out that I am pregnant with his child. To complicate things even more, the lady from the church has come forward and admitted that my husband is not the fa-

ther of her daughter's baby and they had never been together sexually. Now I am pregnant with our nephew's child. What am I to do? Should I tell my husband about what has happened or should I just walk away from our marriage with our two children and start a new life? I know if I tell him, he will flip out. Please help me!

There's enough foolishness for every age group to go around in this letter, From the eighties on down to the twenties! This woman was wrong for taking gossip and rumor from someone in the church as truth. She was doubly wrong for retaliating by sleeping with her husband's nephew. Two wrongs don't make a right. That old lady, the busybody, had no right stirring up all this crazy mess. All I can say is the truth will set you free. Of course her husband's going to be upset when she tells him, but this woman has several choices. She can be truthful, walk away from her family, or pretend that the baby is her husband's. I highly warn against the last two. Walking away is cowardly, and lying about the baby's father is horrible and unfair to all parties involved. So she's gonna have to (wo)man up and tell the truth.

Subject: I Cannot Help Myself!

Hi, Steve, Shirley, and the morning crew,

I am 21 years old and I have a major issue. You see, I am very attractive and I tend to attract a lot of guys. The problem is my relationships never last for longer than six months! I am a very serious college student and I have a lot going for myself, but I always jump into bed too soon with men. This has been going on for at least two

years. I know that I am young but I am also very mature and I want
a partner to go through life with. Steve, I read your book about the
probation period and I took that into consideration. However, I am a
very honest person and when a guy tells me that he likes me and
wants to get serious I believe him. So I let my guard down and have
sex with him and then everything goes downhill. I have considered
being celibate but that is really hard! I don't think I'm promiscuous or
anything, but am I too trusting too soon? I don't want to walk around
like a bitter woman or anything but I really need some help. I even
tried talking to a counselor about this. Can you give a young sister
some advice, because I don't want to get married and have my past
haunt me.

This woman already identified the problem. She's just not understanding what it is. She jumps in bed with these men too
quickly. Whenever you do that, yeah, a man is gonna leave.
Now, she read Steve's book and he has things in there about
standards and requirements and the ninety-day rule. It doesn't
seem like this woman can hold off on sex for nine days, let
alone ninety! A man will not take you seriously if you sleep
with him too soon. She talks about being mature and smart
and beautiful, but I wonder if she has self-esteem issues. She
doesn't seem to think she is worth waiting for. I'm urging her
not to let herself be used and disrespected any longer. Bottom
line, she needs to turn a new page, look at her mistakes, and
stop repeating the actions that haven't worked for her in the
past! If she wants a different outcome, then she needs to
change how she approaches relationships and value herself
more.

Subject: Hating Me!

Dear Steve and Shirley,

I'm 28 and I don't know what to do. I'm dating a man eleven years older than I am and our relationship was going wonderfully until I ended up pregnant! He says that I got pregnant on purpose and that if I have this child I will ruin his life! He had a four-year plan and wants me to get rid of the baby. Mind you, he knew I wasn't on any birth control and he did not insist on using protection! Not just once, but every time we had sex. I don't want him to hate me, because I do love him dearly. But I don't want to put my body through an abortion. Also, I mentioned giving up the child for adoption and he had a fit about that! He has three children who are almost adults and he said he wanted to wait till they graduated before having more kids. I can't stand feeling like he hates me. I'm scared he won't be there and I don't want to raise a child alone! What do I do?

Let me just say this, if this man isn't going to be there for her and the baby after their history, then he's not the man for her. The nerve of him to blame this woman for messing up his life. She didn't get pregnant by herself. He needs to man up and take responsibility for what he's done and help her with the baby. If he doesn't, she needs to take him to court and get child support. It's about the baby now. All babies are blessings, and this man is dead wrong!

Subject: Forget Boyfriend/Baby Mama Drama

Morning to The Steve Harvey Morning Show,

I'm a 33-year-old single mother of one. I work part-time and am a full-time student. I met a guy who has all the qualities that I like in a man: hardworking, has his own place, and a great sense of humor. Things went well for some time, then all of a sudden "it happened!" Baby mama/psycho chick drama! Once his ex found out he was dating someone she started slashing his tires, hacking into his cell phone, being very obsessive toward him, and then took him to court for child support. I spoke to him three days straight. Then all of a sudden on the fourth day his butt had amnesia and could not remember who I was. He was asking me questions like, How did you get my phone number? Where do I know you from? I was shocked and confused. I think that he is back with his son's mother, because of that $550 that he has to pay a month in court-ordered support. The way he is acting I think she put a ROOT on his behind! Should I keep pursuing him or walk away?

This guy is a loser, and if she stays in this situation with him she'll be a loser, too! Yes, of course, he's back with his baby's mama. So, she should chalk the time that she had with him as a life experience and move on. There's no use looking back. Technically this man is free to date whomever he wants, but he obviously can't do it because of unresolved issues with his child's mother. I'm sure there are plenty of guys out there that would love to be in a relationship with the writer of this letter. She should be happy to cut her losses, because the baby mama will not let her have any peace. No one needs that type of drama. Next!

Subject: So Angry I'm Seeing Red!

Dear Steve and Shirley,

I begin this letter by saying I hate my husband of twelve years. I found out he has been meeting women that he connects with online. He doesn't realize that one of the women he is talking to is me. I feel as though he has made a fool of me, and I've been stupid. The thought of him makes me sick to my stomach. When he says, "I love you," I want to say, "Kiss my butt." I don't even care to confront him. For what? To give him the opportunity to tell me another stupid lie? At this moment it is not do I leave but how do I leave and this is why I am writing you. I know getting even is not the right choice but it would make me feel better. I would like your opinion. Here is what I came up with so far: Do I talk to him first and ask him what I am lacking that makes him look elsewhere? Or do I just get my ducks in a row and walk? (By the way, I was thinking about putting a knife through a printout of his online profile and sticking it over his side of the bed while he is sleeping.) What do you think?

She definitely can't blame herself. There could be any number of reasons her husband is doing what he's doing. But I'm concerned because she starts off her letter by saying how much she hates her husband. There are some serious issues here and she needs to take a deep breath and step back. If she feels that she can't talk to her husband about his behavior and see if they can work it out, then I suggest she seek counseling before making any drastic moves. As for the knife over his side of the bed: This woman definitely does not need to be handling sharp objects in her current mind-set!

Subject: Cousin Making the Rounds

Good morning, Steve, Shirley, and the Morning Crew,

My situation is one that is hard to put into words. For years, ever since I was a young girl, I had a crush on my cousin. After growing up and learning from him that he was not actually my "blood" relative we started an intimate relationship. We live in different states so the relationship was able to stay alive for years. The only problem was that he is married with five children. Their marriage fizzled out for reasons unbeknownst to me. After hacking into his e-mail I found out that he has had relationships with quite a few of my cousins. It appears that they were lured in the same way I was—"We're not really cousins." I have saved copies of the many e-mails between my female cousins and this man and posted them to a website for the world to see. I'm considering possibly revealing them to the family at the next family reunion. I'm pretty sure that Shirley is calling me a "hot mess" at this time, and Steve has called me "trifling," and possibly all of us "nasty." That's cool. It is what it is. Here's where I need your advice and/or opinion. Is revealing the letters at the family reunion and to his wife a good idea?

First of all she's right. She is a hot mess, and I'll say it for Steve: This whole situation is triflin'. Secondly, bringing his wife into matters is not a good idea. This woman just needs to get herself together and stop messing around with her playa cousin! It's too bad and too late that she ever sought revenge and too late to change it, because she can't take back the letters that are now on this website. I just urge her not to take this to his wife and their kids. They had nothing to do with this and he is a fool!

Subject: Woman Running After My Pastor #1

Dear Steve and Shirley:

I am writing this letter because I am very concerned about this certain lady that I know wants my pastor. My pastor is a single young man. He is very handsome. A young lady who I invited to my church thinks he is very charming as well, and I know she wants him. She left him a card on his car during service one night. I think they are communicating on the sly. She is very attractive, educated, currently working toward her doctorate degree, and is much smaller than I am. She is a teacher and appears to have money and drives a new car. She is a single mother of three children and her daughter is in college. She is now purchasing a new home. She sings in a gospel group and is very talented. She thinks she got it going on with all those new clothes she wears, but the styles she wears are not appropriate for a pastor's wife. She dresses like she is Tyra Banks or Vickie Winans. She wears all these rings on her fingers. She tries to be more than what she is. She does not attend my church anymore, but when she did, she would always sit in the back. As a matter of fact, I am told by her new church members that she sits in the back of their church and she does not like to talk to them. She stays to herself. I know my pastor is attracted to her, because if I were a man I would be too. As a matter of fact, I overheard a conversation in which one of the men in my church said that she got it going on and if he could he would jump on that. I don't want my pastor with her. There are a lot of single women in my church, and he needs to be marrying one of us. She has her own church. She is a Sunday School teacher and the Youth Director at her church; I am sure she can find a man over there. I discussed this with a male friend of mine, and he said she sounds like the ideal woman to have, but I disagree. He thinks that I am upset and making up all these lies about this woman because I want to be in her shoes. He told me to leave that woman alone, because she ain't messing with nobody. You see, I told the pastor's sisters something about her to cause them to dislike her and to make sure that she would stay out of his life. I am sure it worked because after church they wanted to fight her, but he would not allow them to do so. To me she is a coward, because they were saying all kinds of things to her and she just walked away without saying a word, got in her car, and left. If that was me, I would have threw down. How can I get this woman to understand that the women at my church do not want her with our pastor? As a matter of fact, we don't want our pastor with any woman.

I'll save my piece until after you read this next foolishness.

SUBJECT: *Leave My Pastor Alone #2*

Dear Steve and Shirley:

My church sister has already e-mailed you concerning this lady who is after our pastor. She closed the e-mail before I could put my two cents in. First of all, like my Christian sister stated, this lady thinks she got it going on, but if she feels that she is all that, why doesn't she find a man of her own status and caliber and not our pastor? Our pastor is just a regular and common man. He is not anyone special like you, Steve, or Tommy. He does not need a Miss Fancy Pants like her. He should be with a woman who is housewife material. He needs a homely Christian woman. Not her. We just want her to leave our pastor alone. He does not need a high-class fancy pants woman. Our pastor is kind of country and naive. He would not be

*able to handle a woman like that. Our pastor doesn't even have a col-
lege degree. He hasn't had a woman in years. He has told us time and
time again that he does not want a woman and he does not need a
woman. So why can't this lady understand that? Let her go and screw
her own pastor. His family doesn't like her, and she does not have any
friends. She lives in her daddy's house with her three kids. I am told
that she is purchasing a $350,000 home. I guess she wants to be with
the rich folks now. The only reason she wants our pastor is so that he
can help her pay for that house and that new car she bought. There
are several of us women in the church who live in simple apartments
or houses with little rent and hardly any bills. We do have jobs. Some
of us work at Walmart, McDonald's, and so forth. We can take
care of him. He would not have to worry about paying any bills. We
may not be as educated as that woman or have a good job like her, but
we know how to satisfy him.*

Signed, Concerned for My Pastor

Both of these letters are hot ghetto messes! Why are these
women all up in their pastor's business? The second woman
sounds flat out bitter, because the preacher doesn't want
her! Truthfully, he probably doesn't want anyone up in that
church because they're all messy and bitter. I'm surprised
these women even wrote letters like this. The woman they're
talking about sounds classy and like she's got herself together.
They're haters and they need to stop.

I'm concerned for the first woman's mental health especially. Her pastor can date and see whomever he chooses if he's
not married, right? She needs to stop hatin', too, and leave her
pastor and his personal life alone. All this gossip and nonsense
is not what we go to church for. We go to church to learn

about God and His word and to be better Christians toward our fellow man or woman. Sure, this woman they're beating down may be single, but they don't know what the woman's intentions really are. I guess the only reason they can find not to like the woman is because she looks good and dresses well. Unfortunately, neither woman has even bothered to extend a Christian hand to get to know her. They need to stay out of everyone else's business, especially their pastor's, and tend to their own lives!

ACKNOWLEDGMENTS

To my Heavenly Father, my everything. I listened and I obeyed, and it was quite a relief for me when I said, "Okay, Lord, I hear you." That was the beginning of me writing this book. It's true, I can do all things through Christ, who strengthens me.

To my baby, Sheridyn, you're the best daughter a mom could ever have. I love you so!

To my brother, Andrew "Fish" Clark, I cherish our friendship.

To my family, way too big to mention everyone, but I am yours and you are mine. I love you all!

To my girlfriends, for always holding me down and for your unconditional love. Thanks for not judging me.

To Bishop Kenneth C. Ulmer, for your spiritual guidance and teaching.

To Ms. Shearon C. Smith, for planting the seed so many years ago when you said I should write a book about the Strawberry Letter.

To Mr. Vincent Fudzie, my brilliant, handsome manager, thanks for your wisdom.

To my executive assistant, Myles Culpepper, is there any job you can't do? Thank you so much.

To Elvira Guzman, my publicist, thank you for "staying ready"!

To Rushion McDonald, our super producer, thank you for all your support and love.

To Thomas Miles, aka Nephew Tommy, thank you for your friendship and for making it so much fun to come to work.

To Carla Ferrell, you're more than a co-worker, you're a friend.

To Steve Harvey, thanks for going through this twice before me and showing me the ropes. Now I know you only made it look easy. You inspire me to reach higher and to do more every day. You've truly been a blessing in my life.

To everyone at Softsheen Carson, which has sponsored The Strawberry Letter all these years . . . Thank you, Softsheen Carson!

To our listeners, we couldn't ask for a better group if we wanted to. Thank you all so much. You've been there for us, you've supported us, you've loved us, you've emailed us, you've written some fantastic, crazy, wonderful Strawberry Letters and we just thank you so much from the bottom of our hearts. We couldn't do this without you. So thanks!

Very special thanks to the most amazing editor, Melody Guy. This book would not have been possible without your support, belief, and vision.

Thanks to the agent for this incredible project, Amy Schiffman of Intellectual Property Group.

Many thanks to the wonderful Random House/Ballantine/One World family for your enthusiasm, efforts, and support.

Finally, to Ms. Lyah Beth LeFlore, it's been such a pleasure working with you on this project. Your spirit is so sweet, and free, and giving. We've developed such a friendship and sisterhood, and I got a little sad when we finished this project. Please, let's keep in touch.

And huge thanks to my L. A. glam squad: Tracci Johnson-Merriweather/hair; Angela Johnson/makeup; Linda Stokes/wardrobe; and Logan Alexander/photography. Without you guys I would've looked crazy!!!

In closing, if I've left anyone out please forgive me, and write a Strawberry Letter about it! Thank you, God bless you all, and I love you . . . Bye!

ABOUT THE AUTHORS

SHIRLEY STRAWBERRY is the co-host of the number-one urban radio morning show, *The Steve Harvey Morning Radio Show.* Steve Harvey has dubbed her "the best voice in radio." She started her career in Chicago as co-host of *The Doug Banks Show* then was offered a spot on *The Beat,* KKBT-FM, in Los Angeles. After Radio One purchased the station, she accepted the co-host position for Steve Harvey's new local radio show, which was number one from 2000 to 2005. The show later moved to New York City, becoming a number-one local show there before expanding to a nationally syndicated show in more than sixty markets, with nearly eight million listeners.

www.shirleystrawberry.com

LYAH BETH LEFLORE was the writer for the national bestseller *I Got Your Back: A Father and Son Keep It Real About Love, Fatherhood, Family, and Friendship,* by Eddie and Gerald Levert. She is the author of the novels *Last Night a DJ Saved My Life* and *Wildflowers* and the teen book series The Come Up. Lyah has been a television producer and entertainment executive for more than a decade and has worked at Nickelodeon, Uptown Entertainment, Wolf Films, and Alan Haymon Productions.

ABOUT THE TYPE

This book was set in Monotype Dante, a typeface designed by Giovanni Mardersteig (1892–1977). Conceived as a private type for the Officina Bodoni in Verona, Italy, Dante was originally cut only for hand composition by Charles Malin, the famous Parisian punch cutter, between 1946 and 1952. Its first use was in an edition of Boccaccio's *Trattatello in laude di Dante* that appeared in 1954. The Monotype Corporation's version of Dante followed in 1957. Though modeled on the Aldine type used for Pietro Cardinal Bembo's treatise *De Aetna* in 1495, Dante is a thoroughly modern interpretation of that venerable face.